1996

PAULO FREIRE: PEDAGOGUE OF LIBERATION

PAULO FREIRE: PEDAGOGUE OF LIBERATION

JOHN L. ELIAS
Fordham University

KRIEGER PUBLISHING COMPANY
MALABAR, FLORIDA
1994

Original Edition 1994

Printed and Published by
KRIEGER PUBLISHING COMPANY
KRIEGER DRIVE
MALABAR, FLORIDA 32950

Copyright © 1994 by Krieger Publishing Company

Library of Congress Cataloging-In-Publication Data
Elias, John L.,
     Paulo Freire : pedagogue of liberation / John L. Elias.
        p.   cm.
     Includes bibliographical references and indexes.
     ISBN 0-89464-816-0 (alk. paper)
        1. Freire, Paulo, 1921–   . 2. Education—Philosophy.
     3. Critical pedagogy.   4. Popular education—Philosophy. I. Title.
     LB880.E45   1993
     370.11′5—dc20   92-34530
                                                              CIP

10   9   8   7   6   5   4   3   2

CONTENTS

PREFACE

This book has waited twenty-one years to be written. In 1970, as a graduate student at Temple University, I proposed to write a dissertation on the social and educational philosophy of Paulo Freire. My mentor advised me to include in the dissertation Ivan Illich, the radical social critic. I complied with the request and the result was *Conscientization and Deschooling: Freire's and Illich's Proposals for Reshaping Society*. The desire to publish a book on Paulo Freire was deferred.

Paulo Freire has remained important in my educational work. Many of the courses I teach include lectures expounding and dialoguing with his thought. I have published a number of articles on aspects of Freire's theories. My work in adult education, religious education, and moral education has been to a great degree inspired by his educational theory and practice. What has maintained my interest the most is the fact that Freire is still an attractive thinker for the many Third World and minority students who pursue degrees at Fordham University.

Now appears to be a more appropriate time for such a book. Freire, now seventy years old, is back in his native Brazil. His major work in educational theory appears to be complete. His most recent books are "spoken books" that recount conversations with scholars in which Freire clarifies certain aspects of his thought, responds to criticism, and reveals more of his charming personality than comes through his more academic work.

Interest in Paulo Freire's ideas remains strong among a growing group of scholars. Educators, social workers, health care workers, social and political activists, philosophers, and social theorists are among the scholars that draw on certain elements of this thought.

vii

viii PAULO FREIRE: PEDAGOGUE OF LIBERATION

This book is the first full length treatment of Freire's thought in English to appear since the mid 1970's. My approach is both analytic and critical. My central theses are two. First, Freire's thought is best understood as that of an educational practitioner and theorist. His excursions into philosophy, social theory, political theory, linguistics, and anthropology are controlled by his educational interests. In this way he is most like John Dewey, who viewed philosophy as essentially philosophy of education.

My second thesis is that the most fruitful interpretation of Freire comes from understanding him as a Catholic thinker. Because of his eclecticism, Freire can rightly be interpreted from a number of perspectives. My own view is that it is Freire's religious or theological views on persons, the world, society, and political change that shape many elements of his thought. Freire makes use of many religious concepts and images: Exodus, dialogue, Passover, prophecy, the Word of God, creation, and redemption.

This is also a work of criticism. Through the course of the book I raise many questions about certain confusions, inconsistencies, and possible errors in Freire's thought. These criticisms come from my many efforts to treat his ideas along with the works of other thinkers.

This book first situates Freire's life's work in Latin America and Africa. I present a brief description of his now famous method of conscientization, which is at the theoretical and practical center of his work. I then explore the troubling eclecticism of Freire's writings. Freire's philosophy of persons, society, knowledge, and political change are seen as closely related to his educational interests. Two chapters highlight his education theories; the first details his criticisms of banking education while the other presents the constructive elements of his educational theory. A final chapter makes the case that Freire's work can rightly be considered as an integral part of the theology of liberation which prevails in much of the Third World.

This book has benefited from suggestions and careful editing by James Morgan, a friend and colleague, and Edna Perkins. I dedicate this book to Paulo Freire, teacher of all, especially the oppressed.

John L. Elias
Fordham University

CHAPTER 1

The Making of a Revolutionary

Paulo Freire is probably the best known educator in the world today. No educator in recent history has had his books read by as many persons in as many places of the world as Freire. No educator has spoken to as many teachers, activists, and scholars. He has truly become a pedagogue to the world.

To understand Freire's work and to assess its impact, one must have some knowledge of the context in which he has lived and worked, as well as of the main events in his life. This chapter attempts to provide a sketch of both of these. Within this sketch I will also offer an introduction to his major works. Although no biography of Paulo Freire yet exists, information about him is found in a number of studies, and especially in interviews he has given and in conversations which have been recorded.

EARLY YEARS

The Northeast of Brazil, where Freire was born and where he also developed his basic educational practice and philosophy, is one of the poorest regions of the world. Around the year 1960 the seven state area had an illiteracy rate of seventy-five percent and a life expectancy of twenty-eight years for men and thirty-two for women. In 1956 half of the land was owned by three percent of the population. Only a small percentage of this land is cultivated even to this day. The per capita income was only forty percent of the national average.[1]

Paulo Freire was born in a middle class family on September 19, 1921 in Recife, a port city of northeastern Brazil and a center of

1

great poverty. His father was Joaquim Themistocles Freire and his
mother Edeltrudes Neves Freire. No unusual tension developed in
the family over religion even though his mother was a fervent Catholic while his father was not a practicing Catholic.

In the early years of his life Freire experienced firsthand a
struggle against poverty and hunger when the depression of 1929
struck his middle class family. The family moved in 1931 to Jatatao,
where his father soon died. As a result of this situation, Freire fell
two years behind in his schoolwork, and some of his teachers diag-
nosed his condition as mental retardation. He barely qualified for
secondary school. Freire was deeply affected by this experience of
poverty and vowed because of it to work among the poor of the
Northeast to try to improve their lot.

Freire studied both law and philosophy at the University of
Pernambuco. Although he abandoned for a year the Catholicism in
which he was raised, he embraced the Catholic faith again after
hearing the inspiring lectures of Tristao de Ayade. At college Freire,
like many Latin American Catholics, was introduced to the writings
of the French religious thinkers Jacques Maritain, George Bernanos,
and Emmanuel Mounier. These thinkers would influence Freire's
eclectic philosophy.

After graduation from college Freire spent a number of years
as a high school teacher of Portuguese. In this position he developed
a special interest in grammar and linguistics, which often appear in
his analysis of knowing, learning, and education. Freire's interests
at this time, he tells us, were linguistics, philology, the philosophy of
language, and theories of communication.

In 1944 Freire married Elza Maria Costa Oliveira of Recife, a
grade school teacher and later a school principal, who had been a
student of his. Paulo and Elza worked in Catholic action groups
among middle class families in Recife. Struck by what they saw as a
contradiction between the teachings of Christian faith and the life-
styles of the poor, he and Elza made a commitment to work with
the poor and illiterate. Freire also became keenly aware at this time
of differences among social classes. The Freires have five children,
three daughters and two sons. In his later writings and conversations he often refers to Elza as a collaborator. This was especially
true in his literacy efforts in Africa.

Freire traces the origins of his literacy methods to sessions he
began to hold with parents and teachers while he was a high school

teacher. In an effort to promote critical thinking, he involved parents and other teachers in discussions on such issues as discipline, discipline and freedom, freedom and authority, and memorization.[2] Thus began his lifelong interest in the education of adults.

LITERACY EDUCATOR IN BRAZIL

Following his studies, Freire worked as a teacher and advocate among the people of the slums. It was while he did this work that Freire became involved in literacy training. He gradually began to focus all of his attention on education, especially adult literacy among the poor of Recife.

To make ends meet, Freire worked as a welfare official as well as a director of the Department of Education and Culture of the Social Service in the State of Pernambuco. Between 1947 and 1959, his involvement with adult literacy intensified and caused him to become increasingly dissatisfied with the traditional methods for dealing with illiteracy that posited an authoritarian relationship between teacher and pupil. Freire's additional discovery of a prejudiced point of view within the traditional primer accounts for his refusal to use prepared primers for literacy education.[3] In today's understanding, these primers contained a hidden curriculum consisting of knowledge, attitudes, and values which illiterates were to learn as well as the rudiments of literacy.

In 1959, Freire finished his doctoral thesis on teaching adult illiterates and was appointed professor of history and philosophy of education at the University of Recife. As a professor, Freire maintained his interest in adult literacy and even involved students in his literacy projects.

In the early 1960's Freire plunged into various reform movements in northeast Brazil. A historian of these reform movements, Emmanuel de Kadt, notes that they did not attract a large following, were short-lived, and came to an abrupt end with the fall of President Joao Goulart's government at the hands of a military coup in 1964.[4] These attempted reforms centered around the Popular Culture Movement. This movement pushed for the democratization of culture through discussions on such themes as nationalism, remission of profits, economic development, and literacy. Moreover, students and men like Freire attempted to raise class consciousness and to increase the popular vote.

The early 1960's also saw the rise of rural and urban unions in the Northeast. About thirteen hundred farm workers' unions were founded within twelve months. In 1963, the successful farm workers' strikes in Pernambuco demonstrated the strength of the unions. The first strike involved eighty-four thousand workers, the second, two hundred and thirty thousand. The Popular Culture Movement, together with the Supervisory Agency for Agrarian Reform (SUPRA), had mobilized the workers.

Literacy, however, was key to all the reform movements in northeast Brazil since only literates were permitted to vote. Voting according to the interests of the patrons or owners of plantations had long been considered a political "duty" for peasants. With the formation of peasants leagues under Francisco Juliao in the 1950's, the peasants became more aware of their power to vote. Weffort, in his introduction to the Portuguese version of Freire's *Education as the Practice of Freedom,* pointed out the importance of the literacy movement in Brazil at this time. Weffort also contends that there was a high correlation between illiteracy and socioeconomic stagnation.[5] He charged the power elites of the country with purposely fostering this situation.

This history of Freire's literacy efforts in Brazil is a brief one since the experiment was short-lived. The Popular Culture Movement made use of visual aids to dramatize various issues under discussion. The results were so satisfactory that Freire decided to use the same types of methods with his literacy training. The year 1963 was the actual beginning of the Freire literacy movement. At the outset, the United States sponsored Alliance for Progress was interested in Freire's experiment, which took place in Angicos, a city of the Rio Grande do Norte. Freire received some help from the United States Aid for International Development (AID) program.[6] The results of this experiment were impressive. Three hundred workers learned to read and write in forty-five days.

In the earlier stages of his experiment, Freire worked directly with the Popular Culture Movement, whose leadership was Roman Catholic. Gradually members of the Communist Party infiltrated the rank and file of the movement. It was partly in reaction to this development that Freire transferred his populist method to the cultural extension service of the University of Recife. Movimento de

Base (MEB), another program for literacy training supported by church and government, became radicalized at the same time. This turn to the left only confirmed Freire in his decision to transfer his method to the university.

The year 1962 was a significant one for Freire. The mayor of Recife, Miguel Arraes, placed Freire in charge of an adult literacy effort in the town. Freire used his culture circles, i.e. discussion groups, to promote the effort at adult literacy.

THE PROGRAM SPREADS

When Paulo de Tarso, a friend of Freire, became Minister of Education, Freire's literacy program was extended to the entire nation in June, 1963. A member of Catholic action groups, a liberal reformer, and popular among student leaders, De Tarso appointed Freire director of the national literacy campaign. Between June 1963 and March 1964, Freire initiated training programs for adult literacy educators in almost all the state capitals. There were courses in the states of Rio Grande do Norte, Sao Paolo, Bahia, Sergipe, and Rio Grande do Sul. Freire planned to import thirty-five thousand Polish slide projectors and establish twenty thousand cultural circles in the county to reach the approximately twenty million illiterates. These training courses were developed within eight months, with college students serving most vigorously as coordinators. There were to be thirty persons in each group for a course lasting three months. This national literacy program was modeled after the example of Cuba, which had almost eliminated illiteracy through a massive literacy campaign a few years earlier. It was Freire's hope that the campaign would be as successful as the Cuban literacy campaign had been from 1960 to 1964.

The federal literacy campaign sponsored both the efforts of Freire and the Movement for Basic Education (MEB), the church based endeavor headed by Marina Bandiera. Although Freire's work was separate from from that of the MEB, there was a great similarity between the campaigns.[7] Although the MEB continued on in Brazil under Bandiera's leadership, its government subsidy was cut. It was eventually eclipsed by the government's own Brazilian Literacy Movement (MOBRAL). The MEB prepared a catechism in 1963 entitled *Viver e Lutar* (To Live is to Struggle). It

consisted of thirty lessons which were illustrated with realistic photographs, geared to the experience of peasants and their actual life
situations. The catechism started from assumptions very similar to
those of Freire. From late 1962 onward, a certain amount of give-
and-take occurred, especially in the Northeast, among the various
literacy programs.

Widespread opposition to these literacy methods grew in
conservative circles. Freire was accused of using his literacy training to spread subversive ideas. In an interview, Freire recounted
that the rightist newspaper *Globo,* published in Rio de Janeiro, led
the attack.[8] It attacked Freire for inciting the people to subversion.
The work of the MEB also came under attack, especially its small
catechism.

Incitement to revolt was never the direct objective of Freire as
an educator. Freire wanted only to aid the reformist government of
Joao Goulart in its efforts to bring certain political and social reforms to northeast Brazil.[9] Freire's main interest was democratization. He also rejected authoritarian methods in education, the social
palliative of welfareism, and the stifling of political expression. His
work, however, undeniably contained the seeds of social revolt because it brought the people to a comprehension of the oppressive
reality of their lives. In his *Pedagogy of the Oppressed,* written a
number of years after the Brazilian experience, Freire indeed shows
himself to be concerned with education as a means for promoting
revolutionary action.[10] *Pedagogy* may in fact be considered a handbook for revolutionary education. In proposing this revolutionary
theory, Freire was considering in particular the Brazilian situation,
where revolution appeared to be the only means of bringing about
adequate social and political change.

Freire's literacy campaign came to an abrupt end early in
1964. A bitter political struggle erupted at this time between President Goulart and the military. Goulart had taken over the government in 1961 upon the resignation of President Quadros. Goulart
had long been involved in leftist political reform movements. At the
time of Quadros' resignation, Goulart was on a visit to Communist
China, having already visited Castro's Cuba. The few years of
Goulart's presidency witnessed the most extensive development of
radical and revolutionary groups in Brazil. Although many of these
groups were made up of Marxists, groups of Catholic radicals were
also active in efforts at political reform, especially in the Northeast.

On April 1, 1963, the conflict between Goulart and the military came to an end. The military took over the government. Miguel Arraes, the governor and a friend of Freire, has given a description of the coup and its aftermath.[11] Arraes was one of the persons forced into exile by the new government. Among many reasons given for the coup was Goulart's sympathy with experimenters on the left, such as Freire. Along with many other leaders of leftist groups, Freire was jailed. At the time of the coup, Freire was involved in the literacy campaign in Aracaju, capital of the northeast state of Sergipe. A participant in the experiment described what happened there after the coup:

> About that time, Paulo Freire's shipment of slide projectors arrived for the experiment. The soldiers broke open the boxes, believing they had intercepted machine guns for the revolution. Freire was arrested.[12]

Freire has described the ordeals of his imprisonment, which lasted for seventy-five days. For a period of time he force to remain in a small cage. Though he was not tortured, his ordeal was a painful one.

Freire crossed the line from being a reformist educator to being a radical after the coup in 1964. He realized that reformist activities like those he was engaged in were not adequate to combat the oppressive situations in which he had worked. No doubt the success of the revolution in Cuba had an influence on his thinking, as it had on many leftists in Latin American countries. The success of these revolutions made more apparent the weakness of reform efforts in other Latin American countries. It is probably the case that Freire's evolution from reformist to revolutionary was a gradual process reaching its culmination with the coup of 1964 and his tragic exile. He speaks of his radicalization or transformation as connected with his new awareness that an educator is also a politician. In exile he thought even more about the politics of education.[13]

FREIRE IN EXILE: CHILE

Freire spent seventy days in jail after his arrest. After being taken to Rio de Janeiro for further questioning, he felt that he would be jailed again. So he went into exile with his family.[14] In some accounts it is reported that, together with one hundred and fifty other political prisoners, he was stripped of his citizen rights and sentenced into exile.

With his wife and family Freire went first to La Paz, Bolivia, where he stayed only two months because of the climate and because there were no employment possibilities for him. He then went to Santiago, Chile, where he worked for five years as a UNESCO consultant and with the Agrarian Reform Training and Research Institute (ICIRA). Freire also had some connections with the University of Chile. In Chile Freire directed a national literacy program for the Christian Democrat government of Eduardo Frei. The program was situated in the Department of Special Planning for the Education of Adults whose director was Waldemar Cortes, a principal of a night school in Santiago. In the two years of work there, Freire's campaign won for Chile a UNESCO award for successfully eliminating illiteracy among a great number of the Chilean population. Although efforts were made at that time to establish a permanent bureau of adult education in the country with Freire as the director, these efforts did not materialize, and Freire left Chile to come to the United States.

While in Chile Freire wrote the two books that established him as a leading figure both in adult literacy and radical political education. (Only a brief introduction to Freire's writings will be presented in this chapter since an extensive use of them will be made throughout this book.) While Freire was in prison, he had begun to write an account of his literacy methods. In 1967 he finished this book *Educacao como pratica da liberdade* in Chile, where it was soon published in Spanish and extensively used.[15] This book contains a description of the literacy method which Freire had developed.

Although this book was first published in 1967, it did not appear in English until 1973 as part of *Education for Critical Consciousness*.[16] Unfortunately this work appeared in English only after *Pedagogy* was published. *Education for Critical Consciousness* is a better introduction to. Freire's philosophy and method since it contains a description of the actual method he used in the Brazilian literacy efforts, as well the illustrations which he used in his literacy education. In contrast, *Pedagogy* is a rather theoretical explanation of revolutionary pedagogy. The earlier book also includes his critical essay on extension education in Chile, "Extension or Communication."

Education for Critical Consciousness is valuable for its clear description of Freire's method and for an explanation of the situation in which it developed. It is clear that Freire's main orientations in the book are liberal reformist, Christian democratic, and existential Christian. Freire now recognizes some of his "naiveties" in the book especially those concerning education and politics. The political role of the educator was not sufficiently analyzed. Of this book he comments,

> I began to understand the nature of limits on education when I experienced the shock of the coup d'etat. After the coup, I was really born again with a new consciousness of politics, education, and transformation. You can see this in my first book, *Education for Critical Consciousness*. . . . I don't make reference there to the politics of education. But, I was able to learn after that about history. All these things taught me how we needed a political practice in society that would be a permanent process for freedom, which would include an education that liberates.[17]

Education for Critical Consciousness describes the transition through which Brazilian society was passing. Brazil is presented as a a closed society, lacking in democratic experience. Education is presented as a way of dealing with a massified society in which people are not considered as individuals. Freire describes conscientization as critical reflection which gets at the causes of things. The various phases of the literacy process are described with drawings of the situations discussed in the culture circles. This book, which was written in the context of agrarian reform in Chile, explores the relationship between technology and modernization and attempts to deal with problems that educators face in rural situations.

The short work on "Extension or Communication" included in *Education for a Critical Consciousness* is an important but neglected work. This work presents the theory of knowledge which supports Freire's educational theory. Freire distinguishes between extension programs and programs of communication. Rejecting both idealism and materialism as inadequate to explain human knowing, he describes a dialectical theory which grounds human knowing in praxis. Dialogue, not cultural invasion, is presented as the essence of both education and agrarian reform. This work clearly shows the importance in Freire's educational philosophy of a theory of knowledge.

While in Chile Freire wrote a second book, *Pedagogy of the*

Oppressed, a book which has established his reputation as an international educator. This work, first published in 1968 and appearing in its English translation in 1970, shows Freire to be decidedly more radical than he was in his earlier works. The book outlines a theoretical analysis of revolutionary education. Although many reviewers found it vague, redundant, abstract, and complex, the book has achieved near classic status among books on education. The critics appeared to have lost sight of the fact that the book is more a revolutionary manifesto than a carefully argued philosophical treatise. Many have also criticized the book for its approval of revolutionary violence as the solution to oppressive education and social situations.

The principal themes of the work include the following: Persons to be fully human must become subjects and not be content to be objects. Education should be carried out by and with the oppressed and not for them. Pedagogy of the oppressed entails the conscientization of the oppressed; that is, it should attempt to make them aware of their oppressive situation and show them that through their praxis they can transform this state of oppression. The oppressed who experience violence can resort to violence to liberate themselves. Freire contrasts "banking education" or nondialogic education with problem-posing education or dialogic education.

SOJOURN IN THE UNITED STATES

Freire came to North America in 1969 at the joint invitation of Harvard University's Center for the Study of Education and Development (CSED) and the Center for the Study of Development and Social Change, located in Cambridge, Massachusetts. As a visiting professor at this center he was engaged in seminars and conferences. At this time he came into contact with many North American educators and scholars. Continuing to come to North America almost once a year, Freire has found many sympathetic followers in this country, though he has not been without his critics.

Freire is sensitive to criticism from Latin Americans for having gone to Harvard and other prestigious Western institutions rather than continuing to engage in grass roots educational endeavors. In answer to his critics, he said that he had to see for himself one of the capitals of the capitalist world.

Around this time Freire came into contact with Ivan Illich, a severe critic of schooling in industrialized countries. Freire gave a number of conferences and seminars at Illich's Center for Intercultural Documentation in Cuernavaca, Mexico. Though there are similarities between the two educational radicals, there are also some major differences.[18]

While in the United States, Freire published the most scholarly exposition of his theories. At Harvard he wrote two articles for the *Harvard Educational Review* which were soon published as a monograph *Cultural Action for Freedom*.[19] These articles have been reprinted in *The Politics of Education*.[20] Clearly a Marxist in these works, Freire illustrates the situation of the illiterate in the Third World as one of emptiness and marginality. The theory of knowledge that underpins his literacy practice is given thorough treatment. Dialogue appears as his dominant methodology. In this work his description of conscientization and levels of consciousness receives a strong Marxist interpretation in terms of the effect of infrastructures on suprastructures. The roles of cultural action and cultural revolution are outlined.

GENEVA AND THE WORLD COUNCIL OF CHURCHES

In 1970 Freire moved to Geneva, Switzerland, to work as a special consultant to the office of education with the World Council of Churches, a position which he held for ten years. This position gave Freire entry to educational programs in many parts of the world, notably Peru, Angola, Mozambique, Tanzania, Nicaragua, Grenada, and Guinea-Bissau. Freire's involvement in these countries followed a similar pattern He was invited to countries which had experienced a political revolution, and was asked to aid them in their literacy efforts. Freire was called in as one who could help them mount a literacy campaign which would strengthen the government and the economy.

Freire has not restricted his work to Third World countries. He has also given seminars and symposia in Canada, the United States, Italy, Iran, India, and Australia. In 1973 he was honored for his work by an honorary doctorate from the Open University in England.

In 1971 Freire established in Geneva the Institute for Cultural

Action (IDAC), an organization for study and experimentation with Freire's new method of conscientization. The center produced documents on women's liberation, political education in Peru, and the contradictions concerning foreign aid programs in the Third World.

IDAC was involved in a number of educational efforts in Africa. Freire was invited in 1975 to aid the new government of Guinea-Bissau in its literacy efforts. He directed major efforts in Guinea-Bissau and the Cape Verde Islands. Freire aided the newly formed government led by Amilcar Cabral in its efforts to combat illiteracy. This government has come to power in 1974 by overthrowing a right-wing dictatorship.

The literacy campaign and Freire's involvement in it have been the subject of considerable controversy. Freire has described his efforts in *Pedagogy in Process*.[21] Freire has been accused of implementing a plan that was idealistic and populist and which ignored important political, economic, cultural, and linguistic realities in Guinea-Bissau. The central issue was over the use of Portuguese as the language of literacy. Freire avoided addressing this issue until the last paragraph of the book. He also did not include in the book a letter to Cabral in which he expressed his strong reservations against using Portuguese in the campaign rather than the native languages of the people. Consequently, many have suspected Freire of promoting cultural imperialism or invasion by acquiescing to the demands of the government. Critics have charged that he violated his principles by agreeing to involve himself so deeply in what appears to be a neocolonialist situation. Freire has been questioned on this and has argued that he did what was possible at the time.[22] Freire had to walk the tight rope between being sensitive to the political situation and at the same time aware of the unreality of Guinea-Bissau abandoning Portuguese in favor of one of the many native dialects. In this situation Freire faced the problems of multilingualism, which he had never encountered before.

Pedagogy in Process, a book that documents the literacy campaign in Guinea-Bissau, consists chiefly of letters from Freire to Mario Cabral, Commissioner of State for Education and Culture. The letters, written from January, 1975 to the spring of 1976, reveal a very human side of Freire, which did not come through in previous books but which was known by anyone who met him. His wife, Elza, is shown to be an essential co-worker in this project. In this effort, Freire for the first time connected education with the efforts of governments to increase economic production.

RETURN TO BRAZIL

In June, 1980 Freire was permitted to return to Brazil when President Figueiredo granted amnesties to five thousand Brazilian exiles and dissidents, among them Freire and Miguel Arraes, the former mayor of Recife who had put Freire in charge of literacy education for the city. Freire is presently a Minister of Education in Rio de Janeiro. His wife has since died. Freire has involved himself in the activities of the basic Christian communities in Brazil.

This later period of Freire's life has been marked by a number of publications. In 1985 Freire published *The Politics of Education*, a collection of papers, articles and talks written in the past twenty years. The book reveals many of the areas in which Freire's theories have had application: literacy, agrarian reform, social work, political education, reform of the church, liberation theology, and school systems. The only new piece in the book is an interview with one of his collaborators, Donaldo Macedo. Freire takes the opportunity to rethink his critical pedagogy and to clarify certain aspects of his social and educational philosophy. The intensely human qualities of Freire come through in this interview. He is a man who loves friends, reading, children, receiving letters, music, writing, and eating and drinking. He is "suspicious" of people who prefer pills or plastic food to a good meal, like a Brazilian *feijoada,* or a Cape Verdean *catachupa* or a French dish.[23] For him there is a connection between eating, sensuality, and creativity.

Freire's continuing involvement in literacy is shown in *Literacy: Reading the Word and the World*.[24] This book contains a number of papers and essays in addition to two conversations between Freire and Macedo. The appendix contains the letter detailing Freire's reservations on the use of the Portuguese language in the literacy campaign in Guinea-Bissau. In this book Freire deals with the act of reading and the importance of libraries to promote literacy. Freire takes the opportunity to answer some of the criticisms made of his involvement in Guinea-Bissau. He also addresses the illiteracy problem in the United States. Out of the excerpts from workbooks used for literacy training in the Africa, there emerges a real sense of Freire's commitment to lifelong learning. He also argues for the political potential of this form of adult education.

Freire tackles many issues on education in the First World in a "spoken book" with Ira Shor, an American educator. In *A Pedagogy for Liberation: Dialogues on Transforming Education*,[25] Shor, who has written a number of books espousing a liberating education, converses with Freire on a wide number of topics. What the two have in common is college and university teaching and philosophies of education. Much of the conversation deals with classroom teaching, the main focus of Shor's work.

A deeper penetration into Freire's thought is provided by another spoken book, *Learning to Question: A Pedagogy of Liberation* which details conversations between Freire and the Chilean professor of philosophy, Antonio Faundez.[26] Faundez left Chile in 1973 with the fall of the socialist Allende government and joined Freire at the World Council of Churches in Geneva. He now teaches at the University Institute of Development Studies in Geneva. The two men range in conversation over many subjects: advantages of a spoken book, intellectuals in exile, the role of ideology, educational philosophy, politics and education, and popular culture. The two Marxist intellectuals scrutinize the controversy over Guinea-Bissau. Faundez raises some rather prickly criticisms in the face of which Freire becomes rather defensive.

The works after *Cultural Action for Freedom*, which was published in 1970, do not add anything substantive to Freire's social and educational philosophy, but they supply many biographical details. They show the helpful collaboration of his wife Elza. All of these books make for easier reading than his major works since the translations have been done with great care. Freire sharpens many of his positions and modifies some of them. He admits some of his earlier naiveties and argues with his critics. The intelligence and wide ranging interests of Freire come through in these spoken books. His ideas are controlled by the persons with whom he converses. With Macedo he probes many issues relating to literacy. Likewise, with Shor he relates his theories to the United States context and discusses the possibilities of a liberating education in a country which has become conservative. In his conversation with Faundez he shows his knowledge of neo-Marxist theorists and reviews his work in many parts of the world.

NOTES

1. Clift Barnard. "Imperialism, Underdevelopment and Education." In Robert Mackie, ed., *Literacy and Revolution: The Pedagogy of Paulo Freire*. New York: Continuum, 1981, pp. 12–38.
2. Paulo Freire and Donaldo Macedo. *Literacy: Reading the Word and the World*. South Hadley, Mass.: Bergin and Garvey, 1987, p. 176.
3. Charles Wagley. *An Introduction to Brazil*. New York: Columbia University Press, 1971, p. 192.
4. Emmanuel de Kadt. *Catholic Radicals in Brazil*. London: Oxford University Press, 1970.
5. Francisco Weffort. "Education and Politics." Introduction to Paulo Freire, *Educacao como pratica da libertade*. Cambridge, Mass.: Center for the Study of Development and Social Change, 1969, p. 12.
6. John W. Dulles. *Unrest in Brazil*. Austin, Texas: University of Texas Press, 1970, p. 216.
7. Emmanuel de Kadt. *Catholic Radicals in Brazil*, 1970, p. 103.
8. Thomas Skidmore. *Politics in Brazil 1930–1964: An Experiment in Democracy*. New York: Oxford University Press, 1967, pp. 406–407.
9. Emmanuel de Kadt. 1970, *Catholic Radicals in Brazil*, p. 104.
10. Paulo Freire. *Pedagogy of the Oppressed*. New York: Continuum, 1970.
11. Miquel Arraes. *Brazil: The People and the Land*. Middlesex, England: Penguin Books, Ltd., 1969.
12. Leo Diuguid. Brazil Wages Two-pronged War on Illiteracy: *The Washington Post*, Section D-3, December 20, 1970,
13. Ira Shor and Paulo Freire. *A Pedagogy for Liberation: Dialogues on Transforming Education*. South Hadley, Mass.: Bergin and Garvey, 1987, p. 31.
14. Paulo Freire and Donaldo Macedo. *Literacy*, p. 181.
15. Paulo Freire. *Educacao como pratica de libertade*. Rio de Janeiro, Brazil: Paz e Terra, 1967.
16. Paulo Freire. *Education for Critical Consciousness*. New York: Continuum, 1973.
17. Ira Shor and Paulo Freire. *A Pedagogy for Liberation*, pp. 32–33.
18. John L. Elias. *Conscientization and Deschooling: Freire's and*

Illich's Proposals for Reshaping Society. Phila.: Westminster, 1976.

19. Paulo Freire. *Cultural Action for Freedom.* Cambridge, Mass.: *Harvard Educational Review* and Center for the Study of Development and Social Change, 1970.
20. Paulo Freire. *The Politics of Education: Culture, Power, and Liberation.* South Hadley: Bergin and Garvey, 1985.
21. Paulo Freire. *Pedagogy in Process: The Letters to Guinea-Bissau.* New York: Continuum, 1978.
22. Paulo Freire and Donald Macedo. *Literacy,* pp. 96ss; Paulo Freire and Antonio Faundez. *Learning to Question: A Pedagogy of Liberation.* New York: Continuum, 1989, pp. 103–105.
23. Paulo Freire. *The Politics of Education,* p. 196.
24. Paolo Freire and Donald Macedo. *Literacy.*
25. Ira Shor and Paulo Freire. *A Pedagogy for Liberation.*
26. Paulo Freire and Antonio Faundez. *Learning to Question.*

CHAPTER 2

The Paulo Freire Method: Conscientization

In this chapter a detailed description of the Paulo Freire educational method is presented. It is important to understand that Freire is primarily an educator whose theories are rooted in this educational practice.

Pedagogy of the Oppressed, Freire's best known book, does not present a description of his educational method. Rather, it is a more theoretical book, a philosophical reflection on his educational practice. In it Freire does give details of his postliteracy program which follows the literacy education. For a description of his method it is necessary to examine his first work, *Education for Critical Consciousness,* as well as more recent works that include a description of his literacy work and experience in African countries.

Freire honed his educational method or practice for the purposes of adult literacy training. He also extended the use of this method of postliteracy training or political education.

METHOD OF ADULT LITERACY TRAINING

The Freire literacy method consists of three stages: the study of the context by an interdisciplinary team for the purpose of determining the words to be used in the training, the selection of words from the discovered vocabulary, and the actual literacy training.

Stage One: The Study of the Context

An interdisciplinary team studies the context of activities in which the people participate in order to determine the common vo-

17

cabulary and the problems that confront people in the area. A maximum amount of participation by the people is sought at this level. Their thinking, aspirations, and problems are discussed through informal conversations. The team faithfully records the words and language of the people. Since the method is deeply contextual, Freire developed different lists of words and problems for rural and urban areas in Brazil. Similarly, he used different word lists in Chile and in various countries of Africa.

Freire decided to elicit words from the people themselves because he was against the practice of supplying primers that utilized common words. Freire contends that words should come from the people, that they should speak their own words, and that words are not to be imposed on them. Educators who teach reading in urban areas have come to the same awareness that Freire arrived at in his literacy campaigns.

Stage Two: The Selection of Words from the Discovered Vocabulary

From the words that are discovered among the people, the team chooses words that are most charged with existential and relevant meaning. Freire was interested not only in the typical expressions of the people but also in words that possessed major emotional content and had an impact on them. He called these words *generative* because of their power to generate or suggest other words for the learners.

Freire has various criteria for his choice of generative words for his literacy training. The first criterion is the capacity of the words to include *the basic sounds* of the language being used, mainly Portuguese or Spanish. The words of these languages are based on syllables with little variation in vowel sounds and with a minimum combination of syllables. Freire has found that sixteen to twenty words suffice to cover all the sounds of these languages.

The second criterion for the choice of generative words is that the vocabulary, once organized, would enable the learners to move *from simple letters and sounds to more complex ones.* Freire in this way ensured success for the method by providing a sense of accomplishment at the earlier stages of the training. With the basic words as a point of departure, the learners could discover syllables, letters, and specific difficulties with syllables in their own language. The chosen words, if truly generative, served as spring boards in discovering new words.

The third and most important criterion for the choice of a word as generative is its capacity to generate in people the ability to *confront the social, cultural, and political reality* in which they live. For Freire the words have to suggest and mean something important for the people; they must stimulate both mind and emotions of the participants. For example, some of the words chosen for use in the state of Rio de Janeiro were: *favela*-slum; *terreno*-plot of land; *trabaho*-work; *salario*-salary; *governo*-government; *manque*-swamp (also the zone of prostitution in Rio); and *riquezza*-wealth. Such provocative words sparked discussions about pressing problems in the life of the people: poverty, property rights, distribution of land, the meaning and value of work, just wages, the power of government over people's lives, the evils of prostitution on both personal and social levels, and inequities in the distribution of wealth.

Stage Three: The Actual Literacy Training

In organizing his literacy efforts, Freire attempted to avoid as much as possible both the language and organization of schooling. The group of learners formed not a class but a "culture circle." The leader was not generally called a teacher but rather a coordinator. Dialogue was to replace the traditional lecture or passing on of information. Learners were not to be passive recipients but active group participants. The purpose of the culture circles was to learn reading and writing by either clarifying situations or seeking action that comes from this clarification. Thus the purpose of the training went beyond technical mastery of a language to include change in consciousness and an orientation to action. For Freire:

> Acquiring literacy does not involve memorizing sentences, words and syllables—lifeless objects unconnected to an existential universe—but rather an attitude of creation and re-creation, a self transformation producing a stance of intervention in one's context.[1]

Coordinators for groups were carefully chosen for their ability to understand the life of the people and to engage in dialogue with them. They worked with about twenty-five to thirty persons. The sessions in Brazil met every week night for six to eight weeks.

Motivation Sessions.

When Freire first began his literacy training in Brazil, he engaged the participants in three sessions in order to motivate them for the training. Since he found in Chile that the people were anxious to move quickly to the actual literacy training, he incorporated the content of these sessions into the literacy training. In these preliminary sessions the group coordinator showed slides or pictures unaccompanied by words. The reason for doing this was to provoke among the people some sort of discussion or debate about the notions of persons, world, nature, nature and culture, persons and animals, human culture, and patterns of human behavior. Freire desired that participants recognize the difference between the realm of nature, over which humans do not have much power, and the realm of culture, which humans both create and shape. An additional purpose, unveiled in the last of the ten slides, was the push toward raising group consciousness which would enable the participants to reflect on themselves while engaged in the process of learning and reflecting. For Freire the process of conscientization began with these sessions. It is to be noted that the topics for discussion comprised the basic concepts of Freire's general philosophy of persons and the world.

The images or codifications of culture that Freire used in Brazil were drawn by Francisco Brenand, a great Brazilian artist. Since these pictures were confiscated after the coup in 1964, the pictures in *Education for Critical Consciousness* are those of another Brazilian artist, Vincente de Abreu.[2]

Development of Teaching Materials.

The interdisciplinary team develops materials appropriate to each situation. These are of two types. There is a set of cards or slides that shows the breaking down of words into their parts. The second type of material is a set of cards that depict situations related to the words and designed to impress various images upon the students. These pictures stimulate thinking about the situations that the words imply. Freire refers to this process of developing images of concrete realities as *codification*. Through various pictures, situations in the lives of the people, such as poverty and oppression, are codified or presented in pictorial form.

Freire has given certain guidelines for these codifications.

They must be neither too clear nor too vague. If they are too clear, there would arise the danger of imposing particular views on the participants. If they are too vague, they would serve not as stimulations to thought but as puzzles or enigmas to be solved. This creative use of images or codifications is a distinctive aspect of Freire's method. Codifications for Freire are not just aids in the teaching process; they are rather at the heart of the educational process since they initiate and stimulate the process of critical thinking.

Literacy Training: Decodification.

Each literacy training session focuses around words and pictures. For example, the word *favela*-slum is printed with the picture of a slum in the background. The group begins to break down the codified whole, both the word and the picture of a slum. They also discuss the existential situation of the slum and the relationship between the word *favela* and the reality is signifies. Then a slide is projected with only the word *favela,* which as a generative word is now separated into its syllables: *fa-ve-la.* The family of the first syllable is shown: *fa, fe, fi, fo, fu.* This is also done with the remaining syllables. The people are then led to create other words using these syllables and their families. When the second generative word is shown, they create additional words by using syllables from both words. From knowing five or six words, participants can begin to write brief notes. At the same time they continue to discuss and analyze critically the real context represented in the codifications.

The order in which words are presented is critical. A three syllable word is presented first, with each of the syllables consisting of one consonant and one vowel. The less common and more difficult material from a phonetic point of view is then presented. Third, concrete words are handled before words that are abstract, social, and political.

According to Freire, pictures are to be discussed before the words are analyzed. Great care is given to developing the pictures to be presented to the groups. The order of presentation is first the picture alone, then the picture with the word, and finally the word itself. Words are then broken into syllables, and the group is encouraged to form as many new words as possible from the syllables learned.

During the sessions the participants practice writing and reading aloud. They express their opinions and write these down. They are also encouraged to begin to read newspapers and discuss local issues. The whole process takes thirty to forty hours to complete.

POSTLITERACY OR POLITICAL EDUCATION

While he was still director of the National Literacy Training Program in Brazil, Freire mapped out a postliteracy campaign for those who had already passed through the first stage of literacy training. He was never able to implement this program because of the military coup. Freire did, however, put into effect this part of his method in Chile. *Pedagogy of the Oppressed* presents a further development of this postliteracy phase. Freire's literacy effort in Africa provided new practical contexts to work out this program.

Stage One: Investigation of Themes

In the postliteracy campaign, an interdisciplinary team digs more deeply into generative themes that reflect the aspirations of the people. These themes are found in the tape recordings and notes made during the literacy campaign. The people themselves are involved in the selection and development of these themes. Freire gives an example of a number of themes that might be investigated in Third World countries: development and underdevelopment, dependency, domination, liberation, propaganda, advertizing, and education. Freire also suggests that the various themes be classified according to the different social sciences. For example, the theme of development can be looked at from the vantage point of economics, political science, sociology, religion, and anthropology. This classification according to academic disciplines highlights Freire's use of a university staff of anthropologists, psychologists, and educators.

Stage Two: Codification of Themes

As in the literacy process, various types of representations are used to concretize and draw attention to the generative themes chosen for discussion and dialogue. Both sketches and photographs are employed. The codifications must represent situations with which people are familiar. Like the generative words, the themes must not be too explicit nor too enigmatic. They should be organized in the form of a fan, so that certain themes open up to other themes. The themes should be presented in such a way that the people are led to see certain contradictions in their lives.

Once the team has developed a number of codifications of various themes, they should return to the groups to initiate dialogue with the people on these themes. This material is taped for further study. The coordinator of the group both listens to the people and challenges them by posing certain problems. A true dialogue should take place between the coordinator and the people.

After the initial dialogues, the team makes an interdisciplinary study of the findings from this preliminary use of the chosen codifications and themes. The themes are broken down into various parts. If necessary, certain themes called *hinged themes* may be added to make clear the connections between two or more themes. Not only the professionals but also the learners involved in the process are free to add these hinged themes to be discussed. Codifications are then chosen for all the themes that will be used in the postliteracy campaign.

Stage Three: Postliteracy Process

Now that the themes have been chosen, dialogue on them takes place between the coordinators of the groups and the people. Freire suggests carrying out this dialogue and education through reading and discussion of magazine articles, newspapers, and books, as well as the use of instruction manuals. But the primary emphasis is to be on the dialogues and discussions that take place. Every effort is to be made to ensure that the people are listened to and that their ideas are considered important.

REFINEMENTS IN PAULO FREIRE'S METHOD

The above description of Freire's literacy and postliteracy methods is based on his work in Brazil and Chile in the years 1965 to 1969. Although Freire has directed his attention to many other matters, adult literacy education has remained a central focus. In a 1987 article Freire reflects on his literacy activity in Africa and gives a detailed description of his method as well as of the Popular Culture Notebooks which he developed for this campaign.[3] These notebooks are a series of books and primers used in the campaigns after Freire and his wife Elza were asked by the officials of the newly

formed republic to be consultants in the massive literacy efforts they
had embarked upon.

Literacy Training Phase

Freire's description of the goals of the campaign expresses
clearly his philosophy of literacy education as a broadly conceived
effort to promote a nation's economic, political, social, and technical reconstruction. The themes of the literacy campaign were:

- Comprehension of the work process and the productive act in its
  entirety;

- Ways to organize and to develop production;

- The need for technical training (which is not reduced to a narrow, alienating specialization);

- Comprehension of culture and its role, not only in the process of
  liberation, but also in national reconstruction;

- Problems of cultural identity, whose defense should not mean the
  ingenuous rejection of other cultures' contributions.[4]

Freire's description of the first Notebook, "Practice to Learn,"
shows how he has rooted his method even more solidly in the concrete life of the people. Instead of beginning with the rather abstract
discussions about nature and culture, the notebook begins with practice, that is, the recreational and work life of the people. Given the
need for economic development in the country, the literacy team
chose many words from the sphere of work: plantation, land, product, hoe, sowing, and source.

What Freire adds to his literacy method is the importance of
writing. Participants are encouraged to learn by practicing writing
and reading. Writing and reading are viewed as "inseparable phases
of the same process, representing the understanding and domination of the language and of language."[4]

Freire also emphasizes the coordinator's reading aloud, especially in oral cultures such as Sao Tome and Principe. After learners
have read silently, each should read aloud. All texts that are read
should also be discussed.

The content of the reading passages in the Notebook depicts
clearly the political and economic nature of literacy education:

With the MLSTP (Liberation Movement of Sao Tome and Principe) we are building a society in which everyone participates for the well being of all. We need to be watchful against those who are trying to bring back the system of exploitation of the majority by a dominant minority.

We become independent at the cost of many sacrifices. With unity, discipline, and work we are consolidating our independence. We repel those who are against us and we gather together those who demonstrate their solidarity with us.

You, the colonialists, you were wrong to think that your power of exploitation was eternal. For you, it was impossible to believe that the weak, exploited masses would become a force in the struggle against your power.

You took with you almost everything that was ours, but you couldn't take with you our determined will to be free.[6]

The Notebook makes use of many of the stories which are told by the people, stories that passed from one generation to another. Learners are encouraged to write these stories and to write some stories of their own, even to the point of developing popular anthologies.

The text found at the end of the Exercise Workbook to be used by the people expresses in simple language the goals and methods of the literacy program in which the people have been engaged. It may also be the clearest expression of Freire's philosophy and practice:

You, comrades, have come to the end of this Exercise Workbook. And you have also come to the end of the First Popular Culture Notebook.

By practicing reading and writing, you, comrades, learned to read and write at the same time that you discussed matters of interest to our People. You did not learn to read by memorizing by heart "ba-be-bi-bo-bu," by simply repeating "ta-te-ti-to-tu." While you learned to read and write, you comrades, discussed the national reconstruction, production, health, unity, discipline, and the work of our People in the national reconstruction. You conversed about the MLSTP [Liberation Movement in Sao Paulo and Principe], about its role in the vanguard of the People.

Now, together again, we are going to take a step forward in the search to know more, without ever forgetting that it is by practicing that one learns. Let's know better what we already know and know other things that we still do not know. All of us know some-

thing. All of us are ignorant of something. For this reason, we are always learning.

The search to know something continues in the struggle that continues.

Victory is ours.[7]

Postliteracy Phase

The Second Popular Culture Notebook used in Sao Tome and Principe presents the clearest explanation of what Freire intended as postliteracy or political literacy training. Since Freire's work in Brazil came to an end before he actually began the postliteracy phase, his earlier writings present only a theoretical explanation of this phase. The purpose of postliteracy training is to reinforce what the learners already know and to increase the knowledge needed for participation in national reconstruction. This training also provides more instruction in the grammar of the language.

The Second Notebook begins with an attempt to provoke a debate on the *act of studying*. This act of studying is not confined to school but happens in many places, including the culture circles used in literacy education. It entails a serious, curious, and searching attitude to understand the things and facts we observe. This kind of study demands discipline, sustained effort to create and recreate and not merely to repeat what others say. We study texts by attempting to interpret them.

The second theme in the Notebook is *national reconstruction,* the effort to create a new society, a society of workers. This reconstruction is to be accomplished though greater production on farms and in factories. The key words used to create this commitment are unity, discipline, work, and vigilance.

The third theme is *work and transformation*. A number of stories are used to show how work transforms the world, how the tools of workmanship are works of culture. The Marxist orientation is clearly reflected in the reading:

> In the colonial days, our work was not free. We worked for the interests of the colonialists, who exploited us. They took over our lands and our work force and became rich at our expense. The richer they became, the poorer we became. They were the exploiting minority. We were the exploited majority. Today, we are independent. We no longer work for a minority. We work to create a fair society. We still have much to do.[8]

The next theme introduced, after a study of the grammar of verbs, is a short account of *the struggle for liberation* in which the people are involved. This struggle for liberation is against colonialist exploration, imperialism, and all forms of exploitation. The role of the people as subjects of this struggle is emphasized.

The struggle for liberation has as its purpose a *new society,* the next theme introduced. This society of free men and women is the result of creative efforts of a people. Although the work has begun, it needs to be completed by the work of all individuals who will create this society with the spirit of unity, discipline, work, and vigilance. This society is described in terms of the socialist classless society,

> a new society without exploiters or the exploited. It is a society in which no man, no woman, no group of people, no class exploits the work force of others. It is a society in which there are no privileges for those who work with the pen and only obligations for those who work with their hands on the farms and in the factories. All workers are to serve in the well-being of everyone.[9]

A theme related to the new society is a society in which no one is ignorant of everything and no one knows everything. Further, this society does not accept a separation between manual and intellectual work. The Notebook continues:

> For this reason, our schools will be schools of work. Our children will learn, from very early on, by working. The day will come when, in Sao Tome and Principe, no one will work in order to study, nor will anyone study in order to work—because all will study when working.[10]

Given the importance of economic development in national reconstruction, one can understand the attention given to the *productive process.* This process is explored in readings about natural materials, the means of production, and the social relationship between workers and their products. Participants read about the change in social relationships in the new society. In the colonialist period workers were exploited since owners had absolute power over the land, the natural materials, the raw materials, the tools, the machines, the transportation and the work force. But now,

> when we speak today about national reconstruction to create a new society, we are talking about a really different society, a society in

which the social relations of production will no longer be those of exploitation, but of equality and collaboration between everyone.[11]

The important Freirean themes of *culture and cultural identity* resonate throughout this Notebook. The readings attempt to make the people realize the value of their own native culture in comparison with other cultures. The task of the people is to create a new culture which, while being open to other cultures, preserves the culture of the nation.

The Notebook engages the participants in the very learning process in which they are involved. With readings on the theme of *thinking correctly,* or what is technically called conscientization (the word is not introduced), the people can forge ahead towards national reconstruction that demands conscious participation, action and thought, practice and theory. The Notebook continues:

> To think correctly means to discover and understand what is found to be hidden away in things and in facts that we observe and analyze. . . . To think correctly, to discover the reason for the existence of facts, and to make the knowledge that practice gives us more profound are not the privileges of a few, but a right that the People have in a revolutionary society.[12]

The Notebooks contain other Freirean themes: the planning of practice, the evaluation of practice, the new man and the new woman, and education. It is interesting to note how simply Freire introduces the people to his concept of education. The text states that the new education must be different from the colonial education. This new education is described as:

> An education through work, which stimulates collaboration, not competition. An education that places value on mutual help, not on individualism; that develops a critical spirit and creativity, not passivity. An education that is based on the unity between practice and theory, between manual labor and intellectual work, and for this reason motivates those becoming educated to think correctly. . . . It has to be a political education, as political as any other education; but one that does not try to be neutral. Upon declaring that it is not neutral—that neutrality is, indeed, impossible, the new education affirms that its policy is that of the interests of our People.[13]

CONCLUSION

This description of Freire's educational practice underlines many aspects of his political and educational theory which will be explored in later chapters. Freire's educational efforts are decidedly political. He is not an educator who sees an intrinsic value in education for its own sake. What motivates him is a realization that people's lives in many parts of the world are impoverished. As an educator Freire attempted to respond to this in the way he knew best, by involving the people in a process of critical reflection on their situation.

In reading the passages in the Notebooks it is almost inescapable to conclude that what Freire attempts comes rather close to indoctrination. Freire is true to his principle that there is no neutral education. Rhetorically, he goes too far in proposing clear cut ideological beliefs in the Notebooks. To make a full and fair assessment of this problem would entail a knowledge of just how the training took place. Were the participants free to reject the ideas of the coordinators and the concepts within the Notebooks? Freire does not record any opposition to these ideas. A fuller treatment of this issue of indoctrination is found later in this work.

NOTES

1. Paulo Freire. *Education for Critical Consciousness.* New York: Seabury, 1973, p. 48.
2. Barbara Bee. "The Politics of Literacy." In Robert Mackie, ed. *Literacy and Revolution: The Pedagogy of Paulo Freire.* New York: Continuum, 1981, pp. 14, 158
3. Paulo Freire. "The People Speak their Word: Literacy in Action." In Paulo Freire and Donaldo Macedo. *Literacy: Reading the Word and the World.* South Hadley, Mass.: Bergin and Garvey, 1987, pp. 63–93.
4. Paulo Freire. "The People Speak,' p. 67.
5. Paulo Freire. "The People Speak,' p. 70.
6. Paulo Freire. "The People Speak,' pp. 72, 73.
7. Paulo Freire. "The People Speak,' pp. 74—75.
8. Paulo Freire. "The People Speak,' p. 81.
9. Paulo Freire. "The People Speak,' p. 82.

10. Paulo Freire. "The People Speak,' p. 84.
11. Paulo Freire. "The People Speak,' p. 85.
12. Paulo Freire. "The People Speak,' pp. 87–88.
13. Paulo Freire. "The People Speak,' p. 93.

CHAPTER 3

Freire's Eclecticism: Drinking from Many Wells

It is rare in these days of specialization to find a scholar so in touch with as many academic disciplines and fields of study as is Paulo Freire. His range of discourse and argument has led to many different ways of classifying him: an educational philosopher, a philosopher of knowledge, a social critic, a sociologist of knowledge, an adult educator, a theologian of liberation, and a theorist of revolution. He is more specifically described as a phenomenologist, an existentialist, a Christian, and a Marxist. Two of his colleagues at the Institute in Geneva gave this explanation for the various descriptors applied to Freire:

> The Latin American reader understands Freire because of an experience of political struggle or an involvement in a social movement which has a socio-economic framework. The Catholic reader identifies with Freire's humanist orientation and feels on familiar ground with Freire and the philosophers who have influenced him. The Marxist reader recognizes in Freire's writings a number of contemporary currents which Marxist thinkers (Gramsci, Lukacs, Marcuse) are used to dealing with. The reader who happens to be an educator finds accents of liberation which characterize progressive tendencies in the contemporary pedagogical debates. Only those who are, in part, all of these people at once or who have, in their own history, passed by way of these different "stages" and been submitted to these different "influences" can grasp the totality of Freire's intellectual development.[1]

Trying to label Freire leads to the question of the multiplicity and diversity of sources on which Freire draws. His chief works are filled with many references to and quotations from philosophers,

31

theologians, political scientists, sociologists, anthropologists, historians, educators, and linguistic scholars. Even in his "spoken books" Freire gracefully moves in and out of the works of others. The use of so many sources makes it difficult to determine where the originality of Freire's theories lies. It also makes it difficult to assess the value of the synthesis that Freire has constructed.

Notwithstanding these problems of academic identity and academic sources, Freire has one very clear identity: he is first and foremost a teacher and an educator of teachers. From the age of nineteen to the age of forty-three he was a teacher in Brazil. Since that time he has been a teacher in many countries of the Third and First Worlds. Even today as he has reached the age of seventy, he is a university teacher in Brazil and a lecturer in many countries. Furthermore, through his books Freire has become a teacher to the world. *Pedagogy,* which has sold three hundred thousand copies in the United States, has been translated into many languages. His other books have also gained a wide readership. On meeting him one encounters a person who both needs to teach and who thoroughly enjoys it.

In this chapter my purpose is to clarify Freire's eclecticism by examining some of the chief sources of his ideas. What sense can be made of the fact that Freire draws from so many sources in his writings? What is the originality of the sythesis which he has established? Is there a consistency in his thought? What has been the development in his thought? What is the best way to describe him?

This chapter will present five major influences on Freire's social and educational philosophy: liberalism, existentialism, phenomenology, Catholic theology, and revolutionary Marxism. While not all of these strains are found in each of his writings, Freire does draw on sources in these areas for significant components of his theories.

FRIERE: THE POLITICAL AND EDUCATIONAL LIBERAL

Freire's first work, *Educacao como pratica da libertade,* reveals him as a political and educational liberal, drawing as he does on the works of liberal philosophers, social scientists, and educators. The book does not contain a single reference to Marx or a

Marxist scholar. This liberal stance was no doubt rooted in his work as an adult educator within the university, his involvement with a liberal reformist government, his connection with liberal Brazilian scholars, and his reading of European and North American liberal academics. The early chapters of the book offer a liberal as opposed to a radical analysis of Brazilian society. He argues that Brazil has resisted becoming an open society because of its lack of democratic experience. This lack has led, in his judgment, to the maintenance of a naive level of consciousness. Freire shows an awareness of the existence of classes but does not speak of class struggles. Many of Brazil's problems, he explains, come from understandings left over from its colonial past.

Discussing Freire's eclecticism without reference to his drawing on Brazilian scholars would be half the story. For an understanding of what was happening in Brazil around the time of his educational efforts, Freire drew primarily on Brazilian social scientists, especially Francisco Weffort, Gilberto Freyre, Fernando de Azeveda, and Alvara Vieria Pinto. These intellectuals, who were part of the *Instituto Superior de Estudos Brasilieros* (ISEB), attempted to interpret developments in Brazilian society in terms of its colonial past when the submissive relationship of masters and slaves predominated. An understanding of this society in terms of development in levels of consciousness had been made by Azeveda. It seems that Freire uses the Brazilian scholars mainly to describe what had been the remote and recent past of Brazil, while he recruits European and North American scholars to explain what was presently happening.

At key points in his social and political analysis Freire draws on the work of European and North American liberals. From the French Catholic personalist philosopher Emmanuel Mounier he gleans his extremely important theme of "the humanization of man," which refers to an inherently progressive and optimistic view of human history. Freire identifies the radical position in Brazilian politics with the political stance of Mounier, who emphasized the ability of individuals to shape history and progress.

Like many other Latin American Catholics, Freire found Mounier relevant to understanding the evolving situation in many Latin American countries. Mounier was a critic of traditional Catholicism as well as of European rationalism. He also became interested in Marxist thought after the Second World War. Other themes from Mounier in Freire's philosophy include the following: history has a meaning; in spite of wars and disasters, history is driving toward the betterment and liberation of humankind; science and technology are helpful in this development; and human beings can be the agents of their own liberation. The same Christian optimism that Mounier possessed is found in Freire's philosophy.

Freire's description of Brazil as a closed society moving toward an open and democratic society echoes the classic study of Karl Popper. The split in a closed society is explained in terms of Karl Mannheim's analysis of the power of utopia and hope for social change. What Brazil needs at this time, according to Freire, is the militant democracy described by Mannheim.

Freire's philosophy of education can also be characterized as liberal and reformist. With regard to the role that education should play in society, Freire cites the works of liberal scholars and educators. He cites Mannheim again to establish the basic importance of education for moving from a "massified" society to a liberal one. Criticizing Brazilian education as being overly verbal or theoretical, Freire contends that it should deal with ideas that have relevance in practice, a reference to Alfred Whitehead's discussion on "inert ideas." Citing the French philosopher Jacques Maritain, he argues that education should harmonize a truly humanist position with a technological one. He draws his concept of dialogue mainly from the German existentialist, Karl Jaspers.

Freire's liberal thrust appears in the themes which formed the basis for the discussions in the cultural circles which he conducted for illiterates and others: nationalism, profit remittances abroad, the political evolution of Brazil, development, illiteracy, the vote for illiterates, and democracy. The realization of each of these themes would entail modifications in existing societal structures.

It is clear that the concept of conscientization described in *Education for Critical Consciousness* is similar to Dewey's concept of critical thinking or reflection. Conscientization is defined by:

> depth in the interpretation of problems; by the substitution of causal principles for magical explanations; by the testing of one's own findings and openness to revision . . . ; by refusing to transfer responsibility; by rejecting passive positions; by soundness of argumentation; by the practice of dialogue rather than polemics . . . ; by accepting what is valid in both old and new.[2]

Though Freire does not cite Dewey, he does defend himself from charges that he has plagiarized the liberal ideas of Dewey and other North American educators.

Although Freire has offered some criticisms of this earlier work, especially with regard to his discussion of the connection between politics and education, he never completely abandoned some elements of the liberal reformist positions in this work. His liberal criticism of society in terms of open and closed is made more specific by his adoption of the Marxist analysis of class struggles, oppression, and domination. His radicalism goes beyond that of the French personalists.

Freire's use of his educational methods has usually been in situations where he has been involved with a government in power, e.g., Brazil, Chile, Guinea-Bissau, and Nicaragua. He has not used his methods in situations which were prerevolutionary. As noted in the last chapter, his original work in Brazil was on behalf of a reformist government. Freire has not actually used his methods to bring about revolutionary changes in political structures. His revolutionary pedagogy has found little application, as such. This accounts for the continuing importance of the liberal or democratic interpretation of his educational theories. When Freire engages in conversations with Ira Shor about educational changes needed in schools and colleges in the United States, he returns to many of his earlier reformist positions, attempting to deal with what is possible in the particular situation.[3]

EXISTENTIALISM

In all of his writings Freire shows his great indebtedness to French and German existentialists. He cites the writings of Gabriel Marcel, Jean Paul Sartre, Karl Jaspers, and Martin Buber.

Existentialist themes appear in Freire's earliest work, *Education for Critical Consciousness*. Here he draws on the existentialist distinction, developed by Karl Jaspers and others, between *to live* and *to exist* to explain the difference between humans and animals.[4] To exist means to transcend, discern, and enter into dialogue. Freire employs this distinction also in explaining the various levels of personal and social consciousness and the purposes of conscientization. From Marcel, Freire draws a great deal of his description of a massified society.[5] For the concept of dialogue based on love, humility, hope, faith, and trust as key to creating a critical attitude, Freire draws on Jaspers. He also utilizes Jaspers's concept of antidialogue to explain the educational method that does not communicate but only issues communiques.[6]

Existentialist themes are articulated by Freire in *Pedagogy*. He recognizes that his concept of banking education is similar to Sartre's concept of "digestive" or "nutritive" education, according to which students are fed by the teacher to fill them out.[7] He follows Sartre's line of thought for his discussion of the relationship between consciousness and the world.[8] The important concept of limit situation, as something to be overcome, is carried over from Jaspers without the pessimism of the German existentialist.[9] Freire's explanation of dialogic action draws on Buber's classic description of I and Thou.[10]

Existentialist themes continue in what is perhaps Freire's most scholarly work, *Cultural Action for Freedom,* a collection of articles which first appeared in *Harvard Educational Review* and are now reprinted in *Politics of Education.*[11] Sartre's concept of nutritive education, as consisting of controlled readings, lectures, memorization, predigested notes, and evaluation, serves as a backdrop to highlight the faults of education in the Third World. Likewise, Sartre is the source for Freire's discussion of the tension between subjectivity and objectivity.

Although Eric Fromm is usually classified as a psychologist, his brand of psychoanalysis brings him close to existentialist philosophy. Freire knew Fromm personally and derived a number of key analyses from him. In analyzing the nature of oppression and dominated consciousness he echoes Fromm's concept of fear of freedom as well as his notion of sadistic love or necrophilia.[12] He also utilizes Fromm's concept that the oppressed people must manifest their love for freedom by a love of life. Dependent as he is on psychologists for his understanding of oppression, Freire perhaps overpsychologizes the term. He never quite moves to the Marxist analysis of oppression in economic and political terms.

In summary then, the Freirean themes coming from existentialism include the distinction between authentic and inauthentic modes of existence and education, the freedom of humans to become subjects, and especially the emphasis on dialogue as the heart of human life and education. Undoubtedly, the main theme taken from the existentialists is the importance of human freedom and dialogue for authentic life and education. Like the existentialists, Freire is concerned that people do not perceive themselves as determined by outside forces in their life situations. Both Freire and the existentialists want people to become aware and to be able to use their freedom of choice to become authentic persons and to work for free societies.

PHENOMENOLOGY

In his analysis of knowledge, an essential aspect of his philosophy, Freire has an indebtedness to European phenomenologists, who are closely associated with existentialists. He is deeply involved in describing stages of human consciousness and the process of changing consciousness. He accepts the principle that exploration of consciousness is necessary for knowledge of reality, since this exploration enables the knower to study the reality that appears to the perceiving subject. Freire unveils reality by investigating both it and the process of becoming conscious of it. Through this method persons become aware that, though they are parts of reality, they are also in significant ways distinct from it. Freire's extensive probing of consciousness leads him to accept some degree of social conditioning of human consciousness as well as the power of human subjects to act on their own to change reality. The charge of idealism leveled against this theory of knowing is discussed in a later chapter.

The influence of phenomenology is quite apparent in the analyses found in *Pedagogy*. Freire's examination of persons as centers of consciousness hinges upon Hegel's study on the phenomenology of the mind, as does his study of the consciousness of the master and the oppressed.[13] Freire uses an extensive quote from Husserl to explain how objects in our environment become objects of our cognition.[14]

Liberalism, existentialism, and phenomenology play important roles in shaping Freire's philosophical orientation. Yet what defines Freire most clearly are his religious or theological vision and his Marxism. The two intertwine to such a degree that, as noted in the last chapter, the more theological he has become the more Marxist he has become.

FREIRE'S RELIGIOUS VISION

Freire was raised as a Catholic in Recife and has spoken of his life long effort to become more Catholic. This religious dimension touches most of his works. On a number of occasions he has related his work specifically to religious and theological concerns. Theologians have had a special interest in Freire's ideas, as will be explained in chapter ten.

Freire quotes religious sources with ease in his first work, *Education for Critical Consciousness*. Freire identifies himself with the ideas of the French Christian personalist, Emmanuel Mounier, who argued for the meaning of the history of the world and of human beings. In Mounier's article on Christianity and progress he also contends that human history reveals progress, which is human liberation. This liberation, which is connected with advances in science and technology, depends on the action of persons. Thus from his earliest writings Freire espouses a view of human history in which God is active through persons to enable them to strive for true human liberation.

In a passage found in the original version but unfortunately omitted from the English translation, Freire describes the spiritual and transcendent nature of persons, which is rooted in their relationship to the Creator, a relationship which accounts for the essential religious nature of human persons. Freire affirms a belief in God and speaks of human relationships to God as central to his view of persons in the world. The relationship that humans should have with others and the relationships that should exist in society are determined by and modeled after the relationship that persons have to their Creator.

> God's relationship over us is based on the fact of our finitude and our knowledge of this finitude. For we are incomplete beings, and the completion of our incompleteness is encountered in our relationships with our Creator, a relationship which, by its very nature, can never be a relationship of domination or domestication, but is always a relationship of liberation. Thus religion (from *religare*—to bind) which incarnates this transcendent relationship among humans should never be an instrument of alienation. Precisely because humans are finite and indigent beings, in this transcendence through love, humans have their return to their source, who liberates them.[15]

This important citation, expressing as it does profound religious truth, will be analyzed in a later chapter. Freire also muses about human existence as a "dynamic concept, implying eternal dialogue between man and man, between man and the world, between man and his Creator. It is this dialogue which makes of man an historical being."[16]

In expressing his vision of persons in the world Freire makes references to other religious sources. That the churches should be involved in efforts to better society is a principle he supports by a reference to the social encyclicals of Pope John XXIII. His optimistic view of the possibilities of human evolution is akin to the theories of Teilhard de Chardin. This view is balanced with a reference to the Christian realism of Reinhold Niebuhr. As already mentioned, his concept of human persons is indebted to the Christian personalism of Mounier.

In writing of the assistance that should be given to nations such as Brazil which are in transition, Freire quotes the encyclical letter of Pope John XXIII, *Christianity and Social Progress,* to the point that such aid should not be be a disguised form of domination but given with the goal of making it possible for nations to develop themselves socially and economically. Many in Latin America were encouraged by the social teachings of this charismatic Pope in their efforts to bring about structural changes in society.

In describing magical consciousness Freire takes a number of examples from magical or superstitious religious beliefs of people, especially peasants. He takes care to distinguish in his writings true religious beliefs from these false beliefs of popular piety.

Religious sources and references appear also in *Pedagogy.* In this book, written to describe and propose the revolutionary character of education, Freire recognizes the fact that his readership will include both Christians and Marxists and anticipates that both groups will find some things objectionable in the book, which he has clearly written for radicals.

The language of *Pedagogy* has a certain religious ring or quality to it. Freire uses such religiously evocative language as vocation, ontological vocation, faith, trust, humility, hope, guilt, conversion, and original sin. Dialogue, which is central to revolutionary education, is to be founded on love, humility, and faith, a description that comes from the Karl Jaspers, the religious existentialist. Further, dialogue is expressed and explained in terms of Buber's I and Thou relationship.

When dealing with the controversial issue of violence Freire cites the work of the Protestant theologian, Reinhold Niebuhr. Freire also depends upon his insights on the spiritual nature of persons and on the failures of the moralistic educator.[17]

In speaking of some myths which oppressed peoples have internalized Freire refers to the myth that oppressors are defenders of Western civilization. He quotes Pope John XXIII's criticism of disinterested aid. He also attacks the myth which holds that rebellion is a sin against God.[18]

Freire expresses admiration for Camilo Torres, a priest, a Christian, and a revolutionary. He salutes the work and the ideas of the French priest, M. D. Chenu, which in effect state that the Catholic church should add to an emotional protest against poverty and injustice an analysis of their causes and a denunciation of regimes which allow them or bring them about.

Thus in *Pedagogy,* a work in which he makes a strong case for a Marxist analysis of society and for Marxist revolutionary action, Freire does not hesitate to draw on many explicit religious sources. As will be seen, in other writings he makes his argument more directly on religious grounds.

In *Cultural Action for Freedom* Freire adopts the ideas of the religious philosopher Teilhard de Chardin to explain the nature of persons as reflective beings. Freire notes that for Christians all lands should be mission lands.[19]

Another key concept for Freire is "speaking the Word." This has deep roots in the Judaeo-Christian tradition through the Greek Fathers, John's Gospel, and the Hebrew wisdom literature. Both literacy and political education are seen as efforts to enable persons to speak their own words.

Besides his major works, Freire has written three articles which are explicitly theological: "The Educational Task of the Churches in Latin America;" "Church, Liberation, and Education," and "A Letter to a Theology Student."[20] He has been interviewed on religious topics. He has also written a favorable review of James Cone's *A Black Theology of Liberation*.[21] In all of these works, he shows how conversant he is with theological concepts and developments. Use will be made of ideas from these works throughout the book. A chapter will be dedicated to a full discussion of his theological views and the theological discussions and controversies his works have engendered.

Freire has shown himself to be a critic of what he considers to be false religious views of God, both as to what God's activity is in the world and as to God's expectations of humans. He is critical of forms of church life and organization. He argues for a radical and revolutionary Christianity.

Freire's theological ideas are similar to ideas of Latin American theologians of liberation. In this theology religion is presented as a force which has the potential for liberating persons and institutions from oppressive elements. Liberation theologians are keenly aware of the role that religion has played in Latin American countries, as well as elsewhere, in maintaining the existing oppressive political and social institutions. They have begun to draw on certain elements in the Hebrew and Christian tradition that point to a more liberating role for religion. It has also been argued that Freire's method of conscientization provides the very theological method for this new perspective.[22]

On a number of occasions Freire refers to the basic Christian communities that are prevalent in Brazil. Freire has spent time talking with these communities and sees his methods as operative in their educational efforts. It is in these communities that Freire witnessed a rereading of the gospel which makes it relevant to life in society.[23] This rereading of the gospel comes about when

> popular groups assume the role of subjects in studying the Gospels, which they no longer simply read, . . . they inevitably study them from the standpoint of the oppressed and no longer from that of the oppressors.[24]

Freire's religious views will be presented in various places in this present work. The essential elements in his religious vision include the following: a view of God as actively involved in the development of persons and in the course of historical events; a view of Jesus as a radical reformer who calls persons to a life of freedom and love; a view of the church as an institution which should be actively involved in opposing oppression wherever it exists; a view of the Christian task as the effort to realize oneself in freedom and at the same time to work with God, fellow Christians, and all persons against oppression.

Though remaining a Catholic and deeply committed to Catholic influence in society, Freire is critical of certain theological tendencies and church practices. As will be seen, he calls for a prophetic church while at the same time criticizing traditionalist and modernizing churches.

Freire thus can be adequately described as a religious reformer. The religious vision which he proclaims has greatly influenced his view of persons, society, politics, and education. It can be debated whether or not he is essentially a Christian thinker who has assimilated Marxist ideas or essentially a Marxist who speaks in religious language and categories to certain audiences. Yet Freire himself explains how Christianity and Marxism are united in him.

A HUMANISTIC MARXIST

Freire has given us an account of his conversion to Marxism. He also makes clear that he did not see his embracing of Marxism as a rejection of his Christian beliefs. He spoke of his conversion in these words:

> When I was a young man, I went to the people, to the workers, the peasants, motivated, really, by my Christian faith. . . . I talked with the people, I learned to speak with the people—the pronunciation, the words, the concepts. When I arrived with the people—the misery, the concreteness, you know! But also the beauty of the people, the openness, the ability to love which the people have, the friendship. . . . The obstacles of this reality sent me—to Marx. I started reading and studying. It was beautiful because I found in Marx a lot of things the people had told me—without being literate. Marx was a genius. *But when I met Marx, I continued to meet Christ on the corners of the street—by meeting the people.*[25] (emphasis in original)

The politics of Freire in *Pedagogy* and later writings is very different from the liberal democratic politics of *Education for Critical Consciousness*. His writings now show the strong influence of Marx and neo-Marxists as well as Marxist revolutionaries such as Mao Tse-Tung, Che Guevara, Fidel Castro, and Amilcar Cabral of Guinea-Bissau.

Freire draws some of his ideas from humanist Marxists such as Erich Fromm and the Polish philosopher Leszek Kolakowski. These men placed emphasis on the writings of the younger Marx.

They expressed a belief in the ideal of human unity and the greatness of human potential, and they exhibited an optimistic faith in the future of humanity. Yet Freire goes beyond this humanist Marxism by accepting such harsh elements of Marxism as the class struggle and revolutionary violence. Freire, however, does not accept the economic determinism that Marx espoused. He prefers instead to stress the cultural dimension of revolution rather than the political and economic. Although this emphasis on cultural revolution enables Freire to make a strong case for the pedagogical nature of a revolution, it prevents him from doing justice to the political and economic factors which are important in all revolutions. Freire's weakness in economic and political analysis have often been pointed out by critics.

A central theme through Freire's work is his analysis of oppression. For this he draws on writers in the Marxist tradition: Albert Memmi, Erich Fromm, and Frantz Fanon. Freire is aligned with these men because he is deeply concerned with the liberation of the consciousness of the oppressors and the oppressed. Both groups must be liberated. Liberation entails dealing with oppressed people's fear of freedom and their tendency to become oppressors once freed. From Fromm he draws his insight into the sadistic nature of the oppressors, which impels them to attempt to exercise total control. He agrees with Memmi that freedom can come about only though revolution.

Freire draws heavily on Marx's epistemology and theory of revolution. In his first reference to Marx he accepts Marx's criticism of the materialist theory of knowledge which states that our knowledge is merely a product of circumstances and education. It is we who transform our circumstances.[26] Freire also notes Marx's analysis of oppression as a force which submerges our consciousness.[27] He cites Marx on human ability to control what we have produced, in distinction to animals. To bring about freedom of the oppressed, Freire, like Marx, sees a need for critical intervention. Revolution for both of them includes change of both consciousness and activity, united in a revolutionary praxis that takes place in the context of a class struggle. Freire, like Marx, focuses on the ideology of the ruling classes as the main obstacle to revolutionary change. His dependence upon Marx also made it more possible for him to accept revolutions even if they were violent.

Both men put great emphasis on the roles of revolutionary

leaders. Since Marx does not seem to have faith in dialogue as part of revolutionary activity, Freire turns to statements of Mao Tse-Tung and Che Guevara to establish its importance. Freire's revolutionary heroes are not widely admired among socialists today.

Where Freire departs from Marx is significant. As mentioned earlier, Freire does not examine carefully the economic bases of power in society and the issue of political power itself. Although Freire clearly identified the problem, he provided no adequate answer:

> If the implementation of a liberating education requires political power and the oppressed have none, how then is it possible to carry out the pedagogy of the oppressed prior to the revolution?[28]

His answer that the class struggle will be resolved by a violent revolution appears to be empty rhetoric, unaccompanied as it is with extensive political and economic analysis.

Freire's commitment to Marxism surfaces in all of his writings after *Pedagogy*. In *Pedagogy in Process* he brings Marx into his discussions about the role of education and politics in the new African republic of Guinea-Bissau. References to Marxist ideas abound in his discussions of revolutionary literacy education as well as in his discussions with Antonio Faundez.[29] Freire on a number of occasions repeats the Marxist critique of schooling, according to which schooling reproduces the relationships and values of the dominant class in society.

CONCLUSION

It appears that Freire defies classification according to our traditional categories. The best that I can come up with is a Christian-existentialist-Marxist educator. First and foremost, he is an adult educator at both a practical and a theoretical level. Everything that he writes has some bearing on education, whether literacy education or political education. His first writings were attempts to understand his own educational practice and the context in which he wrote. The various philosophies he draws on—liberalism, existentialism, phenomenology and Marxism—are in the service of understanding the social context of education, the nature of the person to be educated, the process of education, the relationship between students and teachers, the relationship between education and politics, the nature of knowledge, the method of education, and the role of language in education.

While the eclecticism of Freire is in the sources that he draws on, the unity of his thought lies in the educational philosophy that he forges with these sources as he brings them to bear on the task of education. The understanding of his own experience as an educator is the unifying element in this philosophy of education.

With this view of Freire, one can see the place that religion or theology plays in the development of his educational philosophy. For Freire all education is religious since it deals with the immanent and transcendent dimensions of human life and activity. His Catholicism provides Freire with many of his richest symbols: Easter experience, death and resurrection, love, trust, humility, vocation, communion, and prophesy. Since his philosophy originated in countries which possess a Catholic culture, an analysis of the cultural symbols was essential for him. Freire also incorporates into his Catholic spirit whatever he finds of value in the world of culture and history. He does not make a deep separation between religion and culture, nor between the sacred and the secular. His Catholicism is an integral part of his vision of what persons can become in a world in which they work with God.

NOTES

1. Rosiska Darcy de Oliveira and Pierre Dominique, In Denis Collins. *Paulo Freire: His Life, Works, and Thought.* New York: Paulist Press, 1977, p. 26.
2. Paulo Freire. *Education for Critical Consciousness.* New York: Continuum, 1973, p. 18.
3. Ira Shor and Paulo Freire. *A Pedagogy for Liberation.* South Hadley, Mass.: Bergin and Harvey, 1987.
4. Paulo Freire. *Education for Critical Consciousness,* p. 1.
5. Paulo Freire. *Education for Critical Consciousness,* p. 19.
6. Paulo Freire. *Education for Critical Consciousness,* pp. 45–46.
7. Paulo Freire. *Pedagogy of the Oppressed.* New York: Continuum, 1970, p. 63.
8. Paulo Freire. *Pedagogy,* p. 69.
9. Paulo Freire. *Pedagogy,* p. 89.

46   PAULO FREIRE: PEDAGOGUE OF LIBERATION

10. Paulo Freire. *Pedagogy,* p. 167.
11. Paulo Freire. *Cultural Action for Freedom.* Cambridge, Mass.: *Harvard Educational Review* and Center for the Study of Social Change and Development, 1970; *The Politics of Education.* South Hadley, Mass.: Bergin and Garvey, 1985.
12. Paulo Freire. *Cultural Action for Freedom,* pp. 31, 45, 166.
13. Paulo Freire. *Pedagogy,* pp. 20, 34.
14. Paulo Freire. Pedagogy, p. 70.
15. Paulo Freire. *La educacion como practica de la libertad.* Santiago, Chile: ICIRA, Calle Arturo Claro, 1969, p. 15.
16. Paulo Freire. *Education for Critical Consciousness,* pp. 17–18.
17. Paulo Freire. *Pedagogy,* p. 112.
18. Paulo Freire. *Pedagogy,* pp. 135–136.
19. Paulo Freire. *Cultural Action for Freedom,* p. 16 (footnote).
20. Paulo Freire. "The Educational Role of the Churches in Latin America." Washington, D.C.: LADOC, 3, 14, 1972; "Education, Liberation, and the Church, in Paulo Freire, *The Politics of Education.* South Hadley, Bergin and Garvey, 1985; "A Letter to a Theology Student." *Catholic Mind,* vol. LXX, No. 1265, 1972, pp. 6–8.
21. Paulo Freire. "In Praise of *A Black Theology of Liberation* by James Cone." In Paulo Freire, *The Politics of Education.*
22. Dennis P. McCann. *Christian Realism and Liberation Theology: Practical Theologies in Conflict.* Maryknoll, N.Y.: Orbis Press, 1981.
23. Paulo Freire. *The Politics of Education,* p. 194.
24. Paulo Freire and Antonio Faundez. *Learning to Question: A Pedagogy of Liberation.* N.Y.: Continuum, 1989, p. 66.
25. Paulo Freire. "When I met Marx I continued to meet Christ on the corner of the street," in *The Age* Newspaper, Melbourne, Australia, April 19, 1974, quoted in Robert Mackie, *Literacy and Revolution: The Pedagogy of Paulo Freire.* New York: Continuum, 1981, p. 126.
26. Paulo Freire. *Education for Critical Consciousness,* p. 146.
27. Paulo Freire. *Education for Critical Consciousness,* p. 36.
28. Paulo Freire. *Pedagogy,* p. 39.
29. Paulo Freire and Antonio Faundez, *Learning to Question.*

CHAPTER 4

Philosophy of Persons: Christian-Marxist Humanism

Freire's religious vision penetrates many aspects of his thought. The home from which he came, his experience in Catholic reform movements, and his particular religious world view shape his work and thought. Freire's decade of service with the World Council of Churches broadened his religious perspectives by bringing him into contact with religious leaders and educators throughout the world. This world view can be described as a Christian-Marxist humanism. The Christian vision enables Freire to consider the relationship between humans and a transcendent Being as the norm for judging the relationship that should exist among persons. The Marxist dimension emphasizes the characteristics of reflective choice and the ability to shape history and culture. Although others have attempted to bring both of these strands of thought together, few have done it with the commanding power that Freire has exercised.

While a Christian humanism or personalism is at the heart of Freire's philosophy, he has combined this with existential, phenomenological, and Marxist elements. Freire seems adept at emphasizing different aspects of this coalition, depending on what his audience and subject matter are. This versatility of thought is especially evident in his recent "spoken books" where he engages in lengthy conversations with a variety of questioners. Conversations with an educator bring out his practical philosophy of education. Conversations with an adult literacy educator draw from him a profound analysis of the literacy process. A Marxist sociologist argues with him on the fine points of Marxist socialist theory.

The purpose of this chapter is to examine the humanistic dimension of Freire's thought, to look at what he says about persons in the world. In his writings Freire appeals to a concept of human nature and social reality according to which he shapes his educational and social theories. For him theory is extremely important both for understanding and for shaping practice. Freire terms "true humanization" the goal of education for liberation.

To an educator or social critic a view of human nature and the world is crucial. However, appeals to human nature and reality have to be carefully examined. Assertions that something is good or true without making an argument are often assertions that it is according to human nature or reality.[1] However, appeals to human nature and the real order are not usually appeals to reasons or to arguments, but rather represent a decision to discontinue giving explanations and justifications. Therefore, in determining what thinkers mean by human nature and the world, or discovering in what their humanism consists, one arrives at fundamental assumptions of their thought.

When Freire speaks of human nature, he does so in most optimistic terms. Although he criticizes the oppressive actions that persons perpetuate on others, he is still optimistic about the potential of humans for doing good. Though this optimism may have a basis in his own temperament and disposition, his involvement in utopian thought of both a Christian and Marxist nature may explain the optimism more adequately. Though he is most critical in his judgments of the concrete things that persons have done in the past and are doing in the present, his assertions about the future possibilities of humanity are certainly optimistic.

When Freire engages in philosophical discussions about persons and the world, his language tends to become abstract and vague. He uses many technical terms drawn from his philosophical eclecticism. It is not always easy to get a sure grasp of the precise statements which he affirms, especially in his earlier writings. Although his latter writings, or "spoken books," have a clarity, they lack the depth and philosophical sophistication of his earlier works.

FREIRE'S VIEW OF HUMAN NATURE

Freire may rightly be regarded as a Christian-Marxist humanist. He calls himself a humanist and refers to his philosophy and method as humanistic. He refers often in his writings to the vision of the person that is at the very basis of his thought.[2] Humanization is, for Freire, the goal of every enterprise in which humans engage. In contrast, dehumanization, for him, describes every action that is destructive of true human nature and dignity. This obviously vague and almost tautological description is representative of the style that often characterizes Freire's earlier writing.

Persons cannot be truly human unless they have proper freedom. Human freedom is the condition which enables the completion of the person. Humanization is not primarily an individual goal but rather a social one. Individuals become truly human by their participation in life in society. The Christian-Marxist wedding of conceptions is demonstrated by the fact that Freire borrows from both Teilhard de Chardin and Karl Marx to describe humanization. He borrows the terms "hominize" from Chardin and "praxis" from Marx to describe humanization as the process of combining reflective activity with praxis to create meaningful history and culture.

Freire did not think that a particular vision of persons and the world should be imposed on persons in the educational process. Consequently, Freire strongly objects to the use of primers for literacy education because they attempt to impose explicitly or implicitly a particular vision of humans. The very use of primers implies, for Freire, that learners are beings who are either incapable of or not responsible for making choices about their own education.

Like other educational philosophers, Freire contends that every educational practice is based on a theory of persons and the world. This leads him to his statement on the nonneutrality of education, which has often been cited:

> Educational practice and its theory cannot be neutral. The relationship between practice and theory in an education oriented toward liberation is one thing, but quite another in education for the purpose of domestication.[3]

The most succinct description of his own pedagogical theory, which he describes as a utopian or hopeful pedagogy that has been developed in the Third World, is presented in these words:

> Our pedagogy cannot do without a vision of man and of the world. It formulates a scientific humanist conception which finds its expression in a dialogical praxis in which teachers and learners together, in the act of analyzing a dehumanizing reality, denounce it while announcing its transformation in the name of the liberation of man.[4]

This text depicts Freire's pedagogy. It begins with a *theory* of persons in the world. It is *humanist*, directed toward enabling persons to achieve their true destiny through freedom. It is *scientific*, aimed at a precise understanding of the world. It stresses the importance of *dialogue* between teachers and learners. It involves *praxis* or action-reflection to bring about changes in the world. It is *utopian* in that it entails the denouncing of an oppressive reality while proclaiming a non-oppressive reality. A later chapter will provide a fuller explanation of Freire's educational theory.

As has been indicated in Chapter One, a major source for the thought of Freire is his Catholic Christianity. This influence is evident in his theory of the human person. As will be seen, however, he weaves other strains of thought, notably Marxism, into his fuller understanding of what it means to be human. Yet, though he utilizes various traditions in developing his vision of human persons, the controlling concepts are religious.

Humans, for Freire, are essentially defined by their relationship to God, who has given them the power of reflective and free choice. Humans are best understood as beings of relationships, first of all to God, and secondarily to their fellow humans. Growing through these relationships, they become the persons they are destined to be. For Freire, humans paradoxically must struggle to become what they already are by virtue of the God-given natures they possess. Thus human nature is incomplete, and its completion is to be found in a relationship to God. Involvement in this relationship gives humans a transcendental character. It is this striving for completeness that enables humans to go beyond the limit situations in which they find themselves. As will be seen, Freire extends this capacity for transcendence from individuals to societies. Society's power to transcend itself find its basis in the human "ontological and historical vocation to be more fully human."[5]

GOD AND HUMANS

One dimension of the relationship of persons to God has been explored, the completeness that God provides for humans. Freire also examines the issue of God's activity and human freedom. He argued against the position that God is responsible for social injustice and that humans can do little in the face of oppression if it is the will of God. He explains that an oppressed person

> will look for the causes [of oppression], the reasons for his condition, in things higher and more powerful than man. One such thing is God, whom he sees as the maker, the cause of his condition. Ah, but if God is responsible, man can do nothing. Many Christians today, thanks be to God, are vigorously reacting against that attitude, especially in Brazil. But as a child, I knew many priests who went out to the peasants, saying, "Be patient. This is God's will. And anyway, it will earn heaven for you." Yet the truth of the matter is that we have to earn our heaven here and now, we ourselves. We have to build our heaven, to fashion it during our lifetime, right now. This latter sort of theology is a very passive one that I cannot stomach. How could we make God responsible for the calamity. As if Absolute Love could abandon man to constant victimization and total destitution. That would be a God such as Marx described.[6]

In this passage Freire corrects a distorted Christian notion of humans and their relationship to God by an appeal to an existentialist or Marxist view of human nature. Although the concept of human freedom and responsibility is found within the Christian sources, as well as a belief in the power of humans to change social and political situations, Christianity has at times presented humans as powerless in the face of oppression and poverty. The negative result of such thinking was that satisfaction was found in God's will and in heavenly rewards. Marx hammered away at this position, calling religion the opium that soothes the pains of the suffering and gives them a hope not in this world but in the next. Freire contends that this distorted view was also connected to the peasant mentality in Brazil.

NATURE OF PERSONS: HUMANS AND ANIMALS

One recurrent theme in Freire's writings, which many readers tend to ignore or pass over lightly, is the extended comparison he makes between humans and animals. The comparison is explicit in just about everything that he writes about persons and the world. Freire constantly contrasts the reflection and freedom of humans with the nonreflective and determined existence of animals. He also contrasts the way humans are in the world, as creative and meaning-giving beings, with the way that animals merely exist. In making these comparisons, Freire culls categories from scholastic and existential philosophy. These comparisons accent or color his vision of human nature. Humans are conscious of their own existence. They live not in an oppressive present but in the past, present, and future. They enter into relationships with others. They develop a culture. They are able to take risks.

Though many have tended to ignore this theme in Freire's writings, he contends that it is important and constantly reiterates it.[7] It was this distinction that formed the basis of the preliminary sessions in this literacy process. Freire considered the nonreflective level of existence of many peasants in the northeast of Brazil to be in some ways close to the level of animal existence. He saw the same oppressive present as determining their lives. In these first sessions, Freire attempted to bring the participants to an awareness of the distinction between nature and culture. Nature was the condition of animals, who are determined to repeat again and again the same actions. Humans, however, have a culture, reflect upon what they do, and have the freedom to do things differently. Freire used many illustrations at this stage of the training in order to motivate participants and to raise their consciousness. His codifications or illustrations were designed to do this by showing humans to be beings that enter into relationships with others, form particular cultures, invent better techniques and instruments, transform nature by their work, and reflect upon their developing culture.[8] Freire also made use of these illustrations and discussions on culture in Brazil, but not in Chile where he found the Chileans more anxious to get immediately to the practical task of learning to read and write.

In summary then, the characteristics that make humans what they are include their *openness* to engagement in the world and their abilities to gain objective *distance* from the world, to *transcend* the world, to engage in critical *reflection* upon the world, to *give meaning* to the world, and to *create* history and culture. What distinguishes persons from animals, then, is their distinctive participation in the domains of work, history, and values, all of which are made possible by human freedom.

One criticism can be made of Freire at this point. He takes no account whatever of attempts to show a continuity in nature between humans and animals. He rather quickly dismisses behaviorism as mechanistic and positivistic. In this area, Freire perhaps betrays a dependence upon scholastic philosophy and theology as well as phenomenology. Humans and animals are placed by him at opposite poles. No mention is made of similarities and continuities that exist between humans and animals. The revolution in biology ushered in by Charles Darwin goes without mention in Freire's writings, as generally in neoscholastic thought. He ignores the attempts of behaviorists and other psychologists to show the extent to which many human actions are determined or at least influenced by external factors and unconscious factors. Though a recognition of these aspects of human nature might have tempered the optimistic spirit of Freire's vision of persons in the world, it would have offered a more realistic appraisal of the possibilities for personal and social transformation.

This criticism of Freire is not, as it might appear to be, a minor one. It is my contention that Freire's faulty view of human nature (faulty insofar as he fails to take into account the limitations of human freedom) gives rise to an overly optimistic and simplistic view of the possibility of social and political change. At times, one gets the impression from reading Freire that human and societal change can be brought about simply by willing it. He speaks of this change as if it were merely a matter of seeing its necessity and then willing its existence. At other times, Freire comes through as the religious preacher, urging people to live better lives without showing them how to cope with the personal and societal obstacles that make the living of this life very difficult, if not impossible. Though Freire shows some awareness of the psychological obstacles to human freedom by his reference to Fromm's *Escape from Freedom,* more often he is blind to this dimension and does not consider the many limitations to freedom of action that are present in human existence. A strong commitment to utopian socialism underscores Freire's tendency to exaggerate the power of human freedom.

This philosophy of human nature plays an important part in Freire's thought. Many of his fundamental assumptions are included under the rubric of human nature. His radicalism consists in calling all institutions in society and all human activities into question on the basis of whether or not they foster, in his language, true humanization. His fundamental criticism of traditional education depends upon this concept of human nature as a criterion of judgment. His proposals for a liberating education are consonant with the view of human nature he espouses. His hope for a revolution in society rests in his belief in certain attributes of humans that he deems essential.

FREIRE'S VISION OF THE WORLD

Freire's pedagogy also implies a view of the world. His understanding of the world is tied to his understanding of persons, for persons are always in the world. Though humans and animals inhabit the same physical world, they live in different social worlds. Humans know the world, construct the world, and are able to change to world. For Freire reality is never just simply objective or factual: it also includes our perception of this reality.

In presenting his vision of the world, Freire attempts to avoid two extremes: materialism and idealism. He is critical of materialism, which he calls mechanistic objectivism, for reducing the world to things. He also rejects idealism, which he calls solipsistic idealism, for reducing the world to abstractions. He skirts these positions by describing the world as process. The world that humans know is not a fixed world but one in process. It is a world that humans make through fashioning a culture and living a history. Freire's is the social world, the world of human construct. Though he recognizes that some live in a closed world, a culture of silence, he states that this is not the world that people should know and live in. The fundamental purpose of his educational practice is to free people from this culture of silence. That this can be done, that the world can be changed by humans, is the essential purpose of all human activity.

Humans make a world by saying a human word, by praxis. Freire puts great emphasis on the ability of persons to change the world through their thoughts, language, and praxis. Taken together these create history and culture. Those who do not exercise these powers experience an alienation from the world. Persons become fully human only when they exercise their ability to name the world. They name the world by developing culture and history.

Freire recognizes that the world is a problem or is full of problems. These problems constitute what Freire calls the themes of the world, which comprise a complex of ideas, concepts, hopes, values, and challenges in dialectical interaction with their opposites, striving for plenitude. The concrete representations of many of these ideas, values, concepts, and hopes, as well as the obstacles which impede man's full humanization, constitute the themes of that epoch. These themes imply others which are opposing or even antithetical; they also indicate tasks to be carried out and fulfilled.[9]

The major themes or problems which Freire has identified in Third World societies include oppression, domination, and fatalism. His proposals for literacy and political education are attempts to tackle these themes by freeing persons from negative themes and opening them up to positive themes. To become free from the dominating power of these themes is the essential purpose of conscientization.

In Freire's thought one finds a certain "complementarity," or more properly a dialectic, between persons and the world. Both persons and the world are in process and unfinished. They develop through a mutual or dialectical interaction. The world, that is history and society, comes about through the activity of persons. Implied in this, though not sufficiently stressed by Freire, is that persons are formed by their life in the world of culture and history. The world is valuable only insofar as persons live and do not merely exist in it. To live in the world is to change it through our language about the world and our actions in the world. It is reflection and activity, that is praxis, that give meaning to history and culture, or actually create meaning and culture. The "ontological vocation" of persons, that is the very being or essential function of humans, is to be an active participant in the world (a subject), and not merely a passive object, as animals are.

ANALYSIS OF FREIRE'S PHILOSOPHY OF HUMAN NATURE AND THE WORLD

Though impressive in its hopefulness and optimism, Freire's theory of human nature needs some corrective criticism. A criticism of Freire's Christian-Marxist humanism may be couched in religious terms, as well as in secular language. Religious language is more appropriate, since Freire clearly places himself in the Christian tradition. In Freire's concept of the human person there is little recognition of original sin, the problem of human evil, and the sense of the tragic in human existence. The Christian tradition on human nature, however, is deeply concerned with human evil and sin in the world. It recognizes the sinfulness of human nature. It also proclaims that social structures and institutions may have evils incorporated within them.

It appears that Freire's radical person, who develops through the process of conscientization, will be able to act rationally and in a nonoppressive manner. Freire writes as if the oppressed, once liberated, will be different persons. He seems to assume that they will use their freedom wisely, that they will not be exploitative. Experience tells a different tale. The oppressed once freed from oppression at times become the oppressors of others. What Freire rightfully stresses is that this does not necessarily have to happen.

In his criticism of society, Freire certainly does point out the many evils that persons perpetrate on others. He paints graphically in his own words the oppressive Brazilian society in which he labored for many years as an adult educator. Yet when he describes the person that will emerge after conscientization, this person bears little resemblance to the person who also is capable of oppression. Undoubtedly this is a prerogative of utopian thinkers who proclaim the coming of the new man and woman. It is no doubt the rhetoric of the preacher who proclaims the coming of the Kingdom. But it is a rather narrow base, not only for a criticism of society and its institutions, but also for a program of social and political revolution. The dark side of humans will not be eliminated when the present oppressed are released. Theories and programs of social change must deal realistically with this dark side of human nature. This is precisely what Freire does not come to terms with in presenting his proposals for education and for social and political change. These proposals certainly have value, but only if they are examined in the light, not of a false utopianism, but of a chastened realism.

It seems that Freire is involved in a contradiction. He contends that utopian persons will emerge once persons are released from oppressive restrictions. But who created these oppressive institutions in the first place? If persons could be oppressive in the past, what keeps them from being so now that they are freed from oppressive strictures? The only explanation for present oppression is the dark side of human persons who exploit others when it is in their own interest to do so.

Utopian thinkers like Freire who do not posit clearly described stages of development are involved in a dilemma. If they admit the existence of present evil, they must admit the capacity of persons to do evil and to fashion evil institutions. This negative capacity must be part of human nature. If they deny the existence of present evil, then their proposed utopia already exists, something which Freire certainly does not maintain.

It is not my contention that human nature is so corrupt that any possibility of change for the better is precluded. I do not propose pessimism as an unbalanced alternative to Freire's optimism. My assertion is merely that a complete understanding of human nature demands thoughtful consideration of mountains of evidence that humans do not spontaneously do what is considered good and just, once they are freed from certain restrictions. Giving persons an opportunity to be free is not necessarily a guarantee that they will act responsibly.

The vision of human nature and the world espoused by Freire has been fashioned with dependence upon the religious tradition in which he was raised and educated. It is not, however, in line with that tradition. It lacks some of the realism of the Catholic tradition with its strong insistence upon original sin and human corruptibility. It appears that what Freire has presented as a present or earthly possibility for humans, Catholicism proffers in terms of some future existence. Views similar to Freire's have been expounded within the Christian tradition, usually by religious reformers who eventually attempted to put their views into practice in sects or monasteries. Utopian tendencies, though at times influential in broader communities, usually peter out in smaller groups.

The vision of human nature held by Freire is clearly identical to the vision of transcendent society propounded by utopian socialists. It possesses the same faith in human perfectibility once the deforming institutions of the past and present are removed. Some of the weaknesses of this vision have been pointed out by Heilbroner. He tells us that the deepest weakness of that vision

> has been its failure to formulate a conception of human behavior in all its historical, sociological, sexual, and ideational complexity, a conception that would present "man" as being at once biological as well as social, tragic as well as heroic, limited as well as plastic.[10]

Events in modern socialist states have indicated that these states must always live in fear of the secret "corruptibility" of the people.

The view of human nature articulated by Freire can be aptly described as utopian. As will be seen, the entire thought of Freire is cast in this mold. "Utopian" is not used here in any pejorative sense. Utopianism as a very specific orientation to social change has been discussed by many scholars, including Karl Mannheim, Karl Popper, and Lesczk Kolakowski.[11] These scholars show the utopian vision as a necessary part of the revolutionary vision. Kolakowski speaks of utopia as

> the striving for changes which "realistically" cannot be brought about by immediate action, which lie beyond the foreseeable future and defy planning. Still utopia is a tool of action upon reality and of planning social action.[12]

Though Kolakowski does not specifically relate utopian social thought to a utopian vision of human nature, there is a clear connection between the two. The belief that persons can perfect society rests on the assumption that humans themselves are inherently good and perfectible.

It is difficult to argue against the utopian view of human nature espoused by Freire because one is dealing here with a matter of almost religious faith. Freire asserts that humans are capable of being totally different from what they have been in the past. History does not present this as a viable possibility.

The utopian vision of human nature contains strengths and limitations. It has inspired reformers and revolutionaries to work for needed change in society. It has been a healthy counterbalance to the view that sees all change as impossible. It has enabled humans to break out of present and past institutions. It has been the vanguard of political, social, and religious revolutions.

The limitations of the vision have been well documented. The holding out of impossible goals has diverted people's attention from what can be realistically attempted. The far-off vision has blinded those who hold it to the proper and realistic assessment of present obstacles to the realization of the vision. Human experiments in utopian living have shown clearly that in a short time the new utopian man or woman begins to resemble those they are attempting to replace.

The utopian vision of human nature in Freire leads inevitably to his utopian vision of social change and revolution. It is almost impossible to discuss the one without the other. There is a real sense, perhaps, in which one's vision of human nature and one's vision of society and one's vision of the possibility for change in society can be an integral and coherent vision. Statements about human nature are not statements about some inner essence or being; they are rather statements about what humans do or are capable of doing. Many persons today shun such questions as visions and concepts of human nature. This type of language appears too transcendental and metaphysical. However, Freire belongs to a tradition of thought that expresses itself in such a manner. By speaking in this traditional mode Freire reveals his fundamental assumptions. In grappling with his vision of human nature and the world, we have found that it logically leads to a second dimension of his thought, his social criticism.

Some analysis must also be made of Freire's vision of the world. It is certainly one well-grounded in contemporary philosophy. What the vision needs, however, is some balance from the perspective of the sociology of knowledge. Freire has stated well the possibility of human freedom to create culture and history and thus to change the world. He has not sufficiently attended to the processes by which a history and a culture once established become institutions and thus exercise great influence on persons by socializing them into a particular culture. He recognizes that "a world of culture and history, created by them, turns against them, conditioning them. This explains how culture becomes a product that is simultaneously capable of conditioning its creator."[13] Freire, of course, is more interested in the human potential to change cultures and history. Yet to assess adequately the power of culture to determine and socialize us is a necessary part of a program of social change. A thorough analysis of the social construction of reality demands attention to both processes.[14]

NOTES

1. James E. McClellan. *Toward and Effective Critique of American Education.* Philadelphia: Lippincott, 1968, p. 250.
2. Paulo Freire. *Cultural Action for Freedom,* Cambridge, Mass.: *Harvard Educational Review* and Center for the Study of Development and Social Change, 1970, pp. 5–6.
3. Paulo Freire. *Cultural Action for Freedom,* p. 12.

4. Paulo Freire. *Cultural Action for Freedom,* p. 20.
5. Paulo Freire. *Pedagogy of the Oppressed.* New York: Continuum, 1970, p. 40.
6. Paulo Freire. "Conscientizing as a Way of Liberation." Washington, D.C.: LADOC, 2, 29a, 1972, p. 8.
7. Paulo Freire. *Pedagogy,* pp. 87–90; *Cultural Action for Freedom,* pp. 28–32.
8. Paulo Freire. *Education for Critical Consciousness,* pp. 61–84.
9. Paulo Freire. *Pedagogy,* p. 9.
10. Robert Heilbroner. *Between Capitalism and Socialism.* New York: Random House, 1970, 105.
11. Karl Mannheim. *Ideology and Utopia.* New York: Harcourt, Brace & World, 1966; Karl Popper. *The Open Society and Its Enemies.* Princeton: Princeton University Press, 1983; Leszek Kolakowski. *Towards a Marxist Humanism.* New York: Grove Press, 1968.
12. Leszek Kolakowski. *Toward a Marxist Humanism.* New York: Grove Press, Inc., 1968, p. 70.
13. Paulo Freire. *The Politics of Education.* South Hadley, Mass.: Bergin and Garvey, 1985, p. 30.
14. Peter Berger and Thomas Luckmann. *The Social Construction of Reality.* Garden City, New York: Doubleday, 1966.

CHAPTER 5

Theory of Knowledge: Dialectic and Dynamic

At the center of Freire's educational philosophy is a theory of knowledge or knowing. From his earliest works to his latest conversations, Freire is relentless in explaining all aspects of human knowing: how persons come to know, what knowledge is, how we know that we know, how we exercise our freedom in knowing, what are the limitations of our knowledge, what social conditions determine our knowing, how knowing is related to education, and by what methods we come to know.

For Freire knowing is closely connected with consciousness, becoming aware of the world and ourselves, becoming aware of our knowledge. Both are related to the real world and both are social activities. There may, in point of fact, be no real distinction between the two in Freire's usage.

As is the case with other areas of his thought, Freire does not provide us with a systematic treatment of a theory of knowledge. Yet his treatment of knowing and knowledge is one of the more developed aspects of his thought.

Freire appears driven by his desire to understand what happens in the educational process. This is both a strength and a weakness. It is a strength since an analysis of the educational process of dialogue provides a concrete instance of human knowing. It is also a weakness since he tends to generalize from his interpretation of knowledge as dialogue to a theory of all knowledge.

While in his first discussions of knowledge Freire is under the influence of existentialist thought, in his later writings his ideas are more in dialogue with phenomenologists and especially Marxists. Freire's theory of knowledge or consciousness has undergone devel-

opment. Some aspects of his earliest explanation of knowing in
Education for Critical Consciousness he now considers simplistic or
naive. In later writings, under the multiple influence of Marxists,
phenomenologists, and existentialists, he creates a rather complex
and abstract theory of human knowing. In its most simple form his
theory of knowledge includes these points: First, knowledge is of
the real world. Second, it is what distinguishes us from animals by
making it possible for us to shape culture and history. Third, though
our knowledge is culturally determined, to arrive at critical knowing or consciousness we need to participate in an intentional mode
of education which is based primarily on dialogue.

Although in *Pedagogy* Freire does not substantially go beyond
what he has said in his first book, what he does in later works is
apply the basic theory of knowing to the consciousness of the oppressed and the oppressor. The nature of the dialectical relationship
in knowledge between being informed by reality and forming reality
ourselves is now specified in terms of overcoming the limit situations of domination and oppression. Thus, the coming to an awareness of oppression and the knowing struggle to overcome this oppression provide *the* example of knowing or coming to critical consciousness. Thus, Freire formulates a general theory of knowledge
and consciousness out of a particular form of knowing. One can
also question his repeated statements that through this process one
can arrive at the real nature and causes of reality. This implies a
rather static view of reality.

In his more recent writings, Freire admits some of the errors
in his works, showing that he is open to criticism from others and
engages in self-criticism in order to further clarify his theory of
knowledge.

SITUATING FREIRE'S THEORY OF KNOWLEDGE

In *Pedagogy in Process* Freire presents a description of his
theory of knowledge:

> The theory of knowledge that serves a revolutionary objective and is
> put into practice in education is based upon the claim that knowl-
> edge is always a process, and results from the conscious action (prac-
> tice) of human beings on the objective reality which, in its turn,

conditions them. Thus a dynamic and contradictory unity is established between objective reality and the persons acting on it. All reality is dynamic and contradictory in this same way.[1]

Freire makes the following points in this summary: knowledge is not of ideas but of reality; knowledge has a practical or political objective: education is intimately related to knowledge; knowledge is an active or dynamic process; knowledge entails a dialectical or dialogical relationship between knower and known; finally, since the reality which is known is dynamic and changing, our knowledge of it is dynamic and changing.

Freire stresses that knowledge is of reality in order to avoid the charge of idealism (that our knowledge is merely of our own ideas) that has often been leveled against him. In focusing on the practical, changing, process oriented, and dialectical features of knowledge, Freire assimilates his ideas to the theories of both Dewey and Marx.

In another letter in *Pedagogy in Process* Freire poses the theoretical and practical questions that education as a knowing process poses to us: "What to know? How to know? Why to know? In benefit of what and of whom to know? . . . against what and whom to know?"[2]

Freire rejects both the materialist-objectivist (mechanistic objectivism) and the subjectivist (idealistic) interpretation of knowledge. He rejects the former because of its failure to allow persons any role in the formation of their ideas. (He cites Marx's criticism of this viewpoint.) He rejects the latter because it allows no role for the world to influence our knowing. Knowledge is best described for Freire as dialectical interaction or relations with reality. Freire challenges the Enlightenment view of knowledge since it does not sufficiently consider coming into contact with the world through action. Enlightenment theories are inadequate since they do not attend to the social or dialogical nature of the relationship.[3]

In *Pedagogy* Freire briefly states his overall perspective on knowledge or critical awareness. He states that "neither objectivism nor subjectivism, nor yet psychologism is propounded here, but rather subjectivity and objectivity in dialectical relationship."[4] Through these words Freire attempts to distance himself from extreme forms of objectivism and subjectivism. The danger of the former is in giving too much influence to external factors on human knowing, while the latter cuts knowing off from the influence of these very material factors.

Freire makes the application of this theory of knowledge to education in words that combine his existential understanding with Dewey's experimentalism, though Dewey is not cited:

> If education is the relation between Subjects in the knowing process mediated by the knowable object, in which the educator permanently reconstructs the act of knowing, it must then be problem posing.[5]

Human knowing as critical reconstruction of our ideas about the world through problem posing and problem solving describes well the Deweyan process of knowing.[6]

KNOWLEDGE AND EDUCATION

While devoting a great deal of attention in explaining what it means to know, Freire does not present a theory of knowledge for its own sake. He is not an epistemologist. Freire always discusses knowledge in the context of education. In fact, for him "education is an act of knowledge . . . on the part of the very subject who knows. Education has to take the culture that explains it as the object of a curious comprehension. . . ."[7] Knowledge or education for Freire takes place when individuals recognize a cognizable object in a dialogical and problem posing process. The task of education is to get students beyond *doxa* (mere opinion) to *logos* (true knowledge).[8]

In *Pedagogy in Process* Freire gives a clear explanation of the connection between knowledge and education. He states that "education, cultural action, animation—the name doesn't matter—always implies, at the level of literacy and post-literacy education, a theory of knowledge put in practice and a way of knowing."[9] In speaking of education Freire contends that domesticating education is an act of transferring knowledge, whereas education for freedom is an act of knowing and a process of transforming action on reality.[10]

KNOWLEDGE OF THE REAL

For Freire, to know is to apprehend the real world. The basic factors of knowledge are the relationships between human beings and the world. Likewise, for Freire, there is a distinction between the one who knows and the thing that is known. Though his theory of knowledge may be characterized as idealistic, it is not an absolute idealism which reduces knowing to merely a subjective experience. Freire avers that one of the main ways that individuals relate to the world is by knowing it. Persons "apprehend the objective data of their reality . . . through reflection—not by reflex, as do animals."[11] Through this perception persons discover that they are temporal beings, able to live in past, present, and future. With this discovery comes the awareness that they can intervene in reality to change it. Since we have the capacity to know, we can enter the realm of making culture and history. Our power to know and to act makes us subjects and not mere objects in the world.[12]

Authentic knowledge comes to persons who are in relationships to the world. Freire contends, following Sartre, that "in these relations consciousness and the world are simultaneous: consciousness neither precedes the world nor follows it."[13] Drawing on Husserl he explains how individuals engage in knowing by concentrating on certain elements in their field of intuition and making them objects of knowledge.[14]

KINDS OF KNOWLEDGE

Freire makes a number of distinctions in his discussion of knowledge. He uses the terminology of Plato and scholastic philosophy to distinguish between between *doxa* (opinion, the simple or conscious awareness of things) and *logos* (absolute knowledge, i.e., knowledge of the reasons and causes of things).[15]

In later writings Freire speaks of two moments in the "gnosiological cycle." The first is the production of new knowledge. The second is the knowing of what is already known. "One moment is the production of new knowledge and the second is the one in which you know the existing knowledge."[16] Freire argues against reducing the act of knowing to the act of knowing only existing knowledge. This distinction is important for Freire, since he advocates that education should involve teachers and students in the process of knowing and not merely the process of handing on knowledge or the products of knowing.

In a short essay on "How to Study" Freire illustrates his active view of knowledge. In analyzing the activity of studying he holds that to know what a text means one must enter the sociological and historical context of the text. Studying for him is reinventing, recreating, and rewriting. He comments: "To study is not to consume ideas, but to create and re-create them."[17]

For Freire, knowledge cannot be explained as the reception of content from another. It is not something static. Knowledge is culturally and historically conditioned.

> Knowledge . . . necessitates the curious presence of Subjects confronted with the world. It requires their transforming action on reality. It demands a constant searching. It implies invention and re-invention. It claims from each person a critical reflection on the very act of knowing. It must be a reflection which recognizes the knowing process, and in this recognition becomes aware of the *"raison d'etre"* behind the knowing and the condition to which that process is subject.[18]

When Freire gives a Marxist interpretation of knowledge, he makes a distinction between scientific knowledge and ideological knowledge. Drawing on Althusser, he explains that true scientific as opposed to ideological knowledge of reality demands "dialectical relationships between men and the world, and the critical comprehension of how these relationships are evolved and how they in turn condition men's perception of reality."[19]

KNOWLEDGE AS SOCIALLY CONDITIONED

Human knowing for Freire is culturally conditioned. In his writings Freire describes three levels of human consciousness that are conditioned by the particular historical situation in which individuals live. A semitransitive consciousness, which knows little outside biological necessities, is produced by living in closed societies. A naive transitive consciousness, which knows reality at a superficial level, is produced by a society in transition from closed to open. A critically transitive consciousness, which knows the proper causes of things, is produced in authentically democratic regimes by a dialogical educational effort based on favorable historical conditions. It is only critical consciousness that knows reality as it is.[20]

An example of the influence of social conditioning of our

knowledge is the effect of mass media in advanced technological societies. The media in a mass society determine our perceptions of reality to such a degree that we do not really know something unless we have seen it or heard it through the media. The media present us with mythical explanations of reality.[21]

Another example of cultural conditioning which concerns Freire in *Pedagogy* is the influence of oppression on both oppressors and oppressed. Freire's approach to this problem is through social psychology rather than through economics and politics. The oppressed take into themselves the attitudes that the oppressors have of them. This explains how the oppressed, once freed, often turn into oppressors. The consciousness of the oppressor is formed by the relationships they have had toward the oppressed. It is possible for the oppressors to know differently, but this entails class suicide or going over to the oppressed. This new consciousness will come to them only if they join in dialogic praxis to aid the oppressed.

In another explanation of how consciousness is conditioned, Freire introduces the Marxist concepts of superstructure and infrastructure. The superstructures of society, which were formed by individuals, dominate the infrastructures, the myths and ideologies by which people live. This explains how the dominators control the consciousness of the oppressed, for it is they who have shaped the institutions of the superstructure. Freire also reinterprets the levels of consciousness in Marxist terms, utilizing the categories of changes in political leadership.

THE NONNEUTRALITY OF KNOWLEDGE

In his later writing about knowledge Freire has made something explicit which was always implied in his earlier writings. Although knowledge appears to be neutral, it is not. All knowledge is for the benefit of particular persons and particular situations. Freire stated this clearly when he argued that there was no neutral education. Like critical sociologists of knowledge, Freire is aware that all knowledge serves the interests of particular groups and individuals. This is why a revolutionary education needs to oppose the existing knowledge forms in society. Similarly, for Freire, what individuals in a particular society know is "intimately related to the overall plan for these societies, to the priorities this plan requires, and to the concrete conditions for its realization."[22] For Freire those who define what needs to be known in society make important decisions about the future of that society. In writing to the educators in the socialist country of Guinea-Bissau, Freire comments:

> The definition of what needs to be known for the organization of the programmatic content of education is one of the most important tasks in a society moving from colonial dependence to a revolutionary struggle for its reconstruction.[23]

He advises that it is not enough just to change the content of the program or simply to modify it. What must be done for a truly revolutionary education is to "establish a coherence between the society that is being reconstructed in a revolutionary way and the education as a whole that is to serve that revolutionary society."[24] To make this change also entails espousing a new way of knowing.

A new society needs to develop a new theory of knowledge or education because education, especially in colonial societies, is a class or elitist education in the sense that what is considered valuable knowledge in such a society is the knowledge that serves the interests of a particular class. For this reason Freire advises that it is better to develop a new group of intellectuals in society than to attempt to reeducate the elitist intellectuals. Though such a reeducation is possible, it is Freire's view that the new but developing intellectuals must be grounded in the unity between practice and theory, manual and intellectual work. The new man and the new woman of the socialist society must be those who participate in the productive labor of society that serves the common good, because this labor is the source of the new knowledge in the society.

Knowledge in the new socialist society should not be defined by bureaucratic institutions such as schools. The schools as markets that control knowledge should give way to democratic learning centers, where teachers and learners are actively engaged in learning. Both teachers and learners must be able to define what is to be learned through a dialogic relationship. For Freire, the collective good will be advanced if both teachers and learners define what is to be known.

In this analysis of knowing, education, and production, Freire combines the ideas of Marxists on the social control of knowledge with the democratic education theory of progressive educators. The

objection to intellectuals is a recurrent one among Marxist revolutionaries, repeated in the revolutionary writings of Mao Tse-Tung.
However, no serious attempt has been made to develop such new
intellectuals. This does not detract from the criticism that Freire
makes of the class control of knowledge nor from the methodologi-
cal matters he suggests. What he says about the agenda setting in
education may be true in some areas of knowledge where learners
have the necessary experience upon which to reflect. There are large
areas of knowledge where the role of the teacher must be more
directive.

RELATIVITY OF KNOWLEDGE

For Freire, the quest for knowledge is a continuing one, especially since there are no absolutes. In his first work Freire contended
that "critical consciousness always submits that causality to analysis; what is true today may not be so tomorrow. Naive consciousness sees causality as a static, established fact and thus is received in
its perception."[25] Freire seems to maintain this position in a later
work in which he states that "since knowing is a process, knowledge that exists today was once only a viability and it then became a
new knowledge, relative and therefore successive to yesterday's existing knowledge."[26]

Freire's view on the absoluteness of knowledge is a confusing
one. It appears, especially in early formulations of his views, that we
can come to a knowledge of objective reality, of the nature and real
causes of things. In later statements, like the one just cited, he seems
to accept a relativity of knowledge

Freire has been criticized for the total openness he maintains
with regard to human knowing.[27] This total openness, if taken
literally, leaves one with no criteria for making any judgments,
including precisely the kinds of judgments Freire makes. Freire has
also been criticized for giving no value to tradition and authority.

Part of the difficulty in this matter comes from the nature of
Freire's writings. Since he does not write systematic treatments in
which all aspects of a subject are scrutinized, he has run the risk of
being contradictory. His position is certainly not totally relativist,
nor skeptical, nor cynical. Perhaps a moderate relativism is the best
characterization of his theory of knowledge.

KNOWLEDGE AND ACTION

For Freire there is an intimate connection between knowing and action. He contends that sooner or later our understandings lead to actions and that the nature of the action corresponds to the nature of the knowing. While naive consciousness will lead to naive actions, critical understanding will lead to critical actions.[28]

Another way to explain this relationship is in terms of a praxis dimension to knowing. The passage from opinion to knowledge comes about only through efforts to work and transform the world. For Freire "knowledge is built up in the relations between human beings and the world, relations of transformation, and perfects itself in the critical problematization of these relations."[29] The process of knowledge thus involves dialogue upon the problems which reality poses for us.

Freire again stresses that knowledge is made in praxis by intervention in reality. He writes that people

> will be truly critical if they live the plenitude of the praxis, that is, if their action encompasses a critical reflection which increasingly organizes their thinking and thus leads them to move from a purely naive knowledge of reality to a higher level, one which enables them to perceive the *causes* of reality.[30]

Freire repeats his key idea that "authentic thought language is generated in the dialectical relationship between the subject and his concrete historical and cultural reality." Knowing involves "a dialectical movement which goes from action to reflection and reflection upon action to a new action. To do this the knower must abstract a situation from the world to focus upon."[31]

For Freire to know is to *speak the word,* an action implying reflection and action. To speak the word is to engage in self-expression and world-expression, in creating and re-creating, in deciding and choosing, and ultimately, in participating in society's historical process. Speaking the word must be related to transformation of reality and the human role in this transformation.

When Freire interprets knowledge and action in Marxist categories, he adds a further dimension to conscientization, the need for denouncing dehumanizing structures and announcing a new reality to be created by men and women.[32] This explanation, apparently taken from Kolakowski, indicates the utopian nature of conscientization. Given the reality of the class struggle between the oppressor and the oppressed, to arrive at critical awareness entails the rejection of structures which maintain oppression as well as the imagining and the working for structures which transform society.

Knowledge is not something static but something dynamic. It involves a constant unity between action and reflection upon reality. Our consciousness transforms knowledge, acting on what we already know. By returning to our previous experiences we grasp the knowledge of these experiences.[33]

KNOWLEDGE AND DIALOGUE

A privileged way of knowing or achieving critical consciousness, according to Freire, is through the process of dialogue which involves a relationship of mutuality among persons. Knowledge for Freire thus entails intersubjectivity or intercommunication. He accepts the idea that all thinking and knowing is dialogical requiring a subject, an object which mediates between the subjects, and the communication between the subjects. For this reason, using the language of semantics, Freire rejects the definition of knowledge merely in terms of the relationship between a subject and a knowable object.[34] Also, revolutionary leaders and educators come to know the objective situation, what reality is, when they are acting in dialogue with their students or people.[35]

Freire further delineates the nature of the dialectical relationship through which knowledge or consciousness comes. It is a "dialectical relationship between the determination of limits and their own freedom." He explains how persons learn:

> As they separate themselves from the world, which they objectify, as they separate themselves from their own activity, as they locate the seat of their decisions in themselves and in their relations with the world and others, men overcome the situations which limit them: the limit situations.[36]

They then come to the true nature of reality. The situation is overcome only by concrete action on the world.

PROCESS OF KNOWING

Freire emphasizes that all knowing begins with experience, in his terminology "knowledge made from experience."[37] Every educational effort, even if it is directed toward rigorous academic knowledge, begins with ordinary knowledge, not specialized knowledge.

There are two contexts in the act of knowing. The theoretical context is the dialogue in a knowing setting. The concrete context is the social reality in which persons exist. The concrete context is examined in the theoretical context. This is done through a *codification* which mediates between the two contexts. Using Chomsky's distinction, Freire explains that to know or read or *decodify* a situation one must go beyond the surface meaning to the deeper meaning, that is the social reality. The process of decodification involves a person in a constant reconstruction of former knowledge of reality.[38] This reconstruction entails knowing many of the causes of the realities. This critical knowledge also demands a new and different praxis, for people do not move from *doxa* to *logos* without a dialectical relationship with the world, without reflective action on the world.

Human knowing is critical reflection. This reflection means that persons can engage and have a distance from reality, understand the significance of actions on reality, communicate about this knowledge through language, and interpret a situation in a number of ways. Freire points out that we are beings who know and who know that we know. Although our consciousness is conditioned, we know that we are conditioned.

Freire explains the nature of knowing by connecting it with posing and solving problems. He contends that, "to be an act of knowing then, the adult literacy process must engage the learners in the constant problematizing of their existential situation."[39] These problems must be related to the life of the individuals who are engaged in the knowing process.

ANSWERS TO HIS CRITICS

Among the criticisms that have been leveled against Freire are some that pertain to his theory of knowing. He has been accused of being idealist and subjectivist in his approach to knowledge. He has also been charged with being a reformist in his politics.

Freire admits that in his writings there are certain "naive" phrases which, if lifted out of context, might characterize his theory of knowledge as idealist and subjectivist. He contends that these are the objects of his own criticisms. He denies that he holds "any simple or immodest illusions about reaching a state of absolute critical ability. It seems to me that the important thing is to see which of the two aspects—naive or the critical—is imposing itself as my praxis and reflection gradually develop."[40]

Freire admits his errors in explaining knowing and conscientization in earlier works. He recognizes that he was wrong to think that the moment of revealing a social reality is a kind of motivation for its transformation. He recognizes that he did not attend to the importance of knowing the real world in the process of its transformation. He now realizes that unveiling reality is not a guarantee that reality will be transformed. He also believes he has clarified his theories in *Pedagogy* and *Cultural Action for Freedom,* contending that more mature reflection on his own praxis has brought him to this new consciousness.

When confronted with the charge that idealism permeated his practice in Brazil, when he stated that the process of becoming aware of an oppressive situation would be sufficient for changing that reality, Freire confesses that he did not give sufficient attention to the political character of education and neglected the issue of social classes and their struggle.[41] Freire valiantly attempts to distance himself from the objectivist mechanical position of some Marxist interpreters and the idealist subjectivist position attributed to Hegel. He strenuously tries to avoid this dualism by arguing for a dialectical unity to explain the subject-object relationship in knowing. He says that, "it is only as beings of praxis, in accepting our concrete situation as a challenging condition, that we are able to change its meaning by our action."[42]

One of the problems with Freire's theory of knowledge concerns the connection between the theoretical situation or context of knowledge, e.g., the school or cultural circle, and the concrete context, the actual problem in the world. *Pedagogy* seemed to state that by decodifying or changing the theoretical context one has already changed the concrete situation. Freire argues that there is a close connection or dialectic between the two situations. Authentic praxis demands the unity of theory and practice, of action and reflection. "Cut off from practice, theory becomes a simple verbalism. Separated from theory, practice is nothing but blind activism."[43] If we are immersed in the real situation, we do not have the distance from it to be critical of it. If the theoretical is removed from the real, we will never come to see what the situation really is. Reflection renders our actions more effective.

Freire has reformulated his definition of conscientization in terms of his theory of knowledge and in a way which emphasizes the importance of praxis, thereby avoiding the twin dangers of idealism and materialism:

> Conscientization . . . is the process by which in the subject-object relationship . . . the subject finds the ability to grasp, in critical terms, the dialectical unity between self and object. That is why we reaffirm that there is no conscientization outside praxis, outside of the theory-practice, reflection-action unity.[44]

CRITIQUE

A number of questions can be raised about Freire's peculiar analysis of knowing. Is it an explanation of knowing or an explanation of one way of knowing? What of knowledge by contemplation or insight? Can one every arrive at a knowledge of things the way they are? This is a good theory of knowledge to explain the type of education that Freire attempted to bring to people. Yet the generalizing of a theory of knowledge from this particular form of knowing has many dangers in it. Freire has explained well the practice of education in which he was involved. But in generalizing to all forms of knowing, he reduces all knowing to one particular kind.

NOTES

1. Paulo Freire. *Pedagogy in Process*. New York: Continuum, 1977, p. 89.
2. Paulo Freire. *Pedagogy in Process*, p. 100.
3. Paulo Freire. *Education for Critical Consciousness*. New York: Continuum, 1973, pp. 146–148.

4. Paulo Freire. *Pedagogy of the Oppressed.* New York: Continuum, 1970, p. 35.
5. Paulo Freire. *Education for Critical Consciousness,* p. 153.
6. John Dewey. *How We Think.* New York: Heath, 1910.
7. Paulo Freire and Donaldo Macedo. *Literacy: Reading the Word and Reading the World.* South Hadley, Mass.: Bergin and Garvey, 1987, p. 5.
8. Paulo Freire. *Pedagogy,* p. 68.
9. Paulo Freire. *Pedagogy in Process,* p. 88.
10. Paulo Freire. *The Politics of Education.* South Hadley, Mass.: Bergin and Garvey, 1985, p. 102.
11. Paulo Freire. *Education for Critical Consciousness,* p. 2.
12. Paulo Freire. *Education for Critical Consciousness.* pp. 4–5.
13. Paulo Freire. *Pedagogy,* p. 69.
14. Paulo Freire. *Pedagogy,* p. 70.
15. Paulo Freire. *Education for Critical Consciousness.* p. 99.
16. Ira Shor and Paulo Freire. *A Pedagogy for Liberation: Dialogues on Transforming Education.* South Hadley, Mass.: Bergin and Garvey, 1987, pp. 7–8.
17. Paulo Freire. *The Politics of Education.* p. 4.
18. Paulo Freire. *Education for Critical Consciousness.* p. 101.
19. Paulo Freire. *Pedagogy,* p. 47.
20. Paulo Freire. *Education for Critical Consciousness.* p. 17–20.
21. Paulo Freire. *Education for Critical Consciousness,* p. 34.
22. Paulo Freire. *Pedagogy in Process,* p. 101.
23. Paulo Freire. *Pedagogy in Process,* p. 102.
24. Paulo Freire. *Pedagogy in Process,* pp. 102–103.
25. Paulo Freire. *Education for Critical Consciousness.* p. 44.
26. Paulo Freire. *The Politics of Education,* pp. 114–115.
27. C. Bowers. *Elements of a Post-Liberal Theory of Education.* New York: Teachers College Press, 1987.
28. Paulo Freire. *Education for Critical Consciousness,* p. 44.
29. Paulo Freire. *Education for Critical Consciousness.* p. 109.
30. Paulo Freire. *Pedagogy of the Oppressed,* pp. 125–126.
31. Paulo Freire. *Pedagogy of the Oppressed,* pp. 1, 13.
32. Paulo Freire. *Pedagogy of the Oppressed,* p. 46.
33. Paulo Freire. *The Politics of Education,* pp. 100–101.
34. Paulo Freire. *Education for Critical Consciousness,* pp. 136, 138.
35. Paulo Freire. *Pedagogy of the Oppressed,* p. 84.

36. Paulo Freire. *Pedagogy of the Oppressed*, p. 89
37. Paulo Freire and Donald Macedo. *Literacy*, p. 87.
38. Paulo Freire. *The Politics of Education*, pp. 51–52.
39. Paulo Freire. *Cultural Action for Freedom*. Cambridge, Mass.: Harvard University Press and the Center for the Study of Change and Development, 1970, p. 51.
40. Paulo Freire. *The Politics of Education*, p. 152.
41. Paulo Freire. *The Politics of Education*, p. 152.
42. Paulo Freire. *The Politics of Education*, p. 155.
43. Paulo Freire. *The Politics of Education*, p. 156.
44. Paulo Freire. *The Politics of Education*, p. 160.

CHAPTER 6

Social Theory: Situation of the Oppressed

Freire situated his critique of education and educational theory within a broad analysis and criticism of society. His rejection of traditional literary and educational methods used in Brazil, Chile, and other countries of the world is related to his analysis of the social systems that existed in those countries. His proposals for a revolutionary pedagogy of liberation are suited for countries in which widespread social injustice exists. Freire focused on education because he believed that, since it was important as a force for maintaining existing social structures, education might become the revolutionary force to combat these same structures. Freire proposed his pedagogy of liberation as the instrument for bringing people to an awareness of the cultural contradictions in existing capitalist systems.

There are various ways to characterize the social theory of Freire. His earliest perspective comes from his involvement with Christian democractic principles and can be termed democratic humanism. In later writings his perspective is better described as utopian socialism or democratic socialism. Thus in economics, he is highly critical of capitalism and advocates socialist control of the economy, while in politics he favors a broad participatory democracy.

The social criticism in which Freire engages is based in part, as was his vision of human nature, upon his theological vision and his experience as a member of the Roman Catholic church. More and more this perspective comes from a Latin American liberation theology which includes both Christian and Marxist elements. Marxist

77

elements in his theory are derived from neo-Marxists or humanistic Marxists such as Antonio Gramsci.

FREIRE'S SOCIAL CRITICISM

Social criticism is weakest in Freire's earlier writings. Freire himself now admits that he had not sufficiently considered the connection between politics, education, and society in these works. For example, one of the weaknesses of his analysis of Brazilian society in *Education for Critical Consciousness,* written in 1967, is his failure to consider the role of the church in maintaining the existing low level of awareness of oppressive measures among the people. One would never gather from reading this book that the conservative Roman Catholic hierarchy was one of the forces opposed to the reforms of the Goulart government in which Freire was deeply involved.[1] Also, Freire speaks only in general of "rightist forces" that opposed these reforms and does not examine the social, political, and cultural forces within which he developed his educational method and philosophy.

Freire's analysis in this earlier work never differentiates the various elements of oppression that existed in Brazil at that time. He simply contrasts oppressors with oppressed. To be sure, he does expose certain false religious notions operating in the consciousness of oppressed people, but he never becomes more explicit than this.

At first sight the influence of Freire's religious vision on his social philosophy and social criticism is not apparent. This philosophy is yoked to both phenomenology and Marxism. On the one hand, he is phenomenological in describing the various levels of consciousness through which societies pass on their way to full and critical development. On the other hand, he is Marxist in outlining the conflict that exists between the classes in society, in analyzing the infrastructure that gives rise to societal institutions, and in proclaiming the necessity of a revolution to bring about the radical changes that must come in the societies of the underdeveloped world. *Pedagogy* and *Cultural Action for Freedom* are replete with references to the writings of neo-Marxists and other social theorists who are outside Freire's religious tradition, if not explicitly opposed to it. In these writings, Freire incorporates such Marxist concepts as the class struggle, the necessity of political revolution, and the inevitability of the dialectic or dialogue.

It is my contention, however, that notwithstanding Freire's extensive use of nonreligious sources, his social philosophy is still consonant with a religious vision which he shares with many Christian thinkers, especially radical Christian thinkers in Latin America. In fact, a certain paradox prevails in Freire's case. As he has become more Marxist, the theological inspiration of his social philosophy has become more explicit. The more Marxist he has become, the closer he has moved to liberation theology.

In *Education for Critical Consciousness*, Freire proposed a social philosophy based on principles of Christian democracy. This book recounts Freire's efforts to implement some of the reforms of the Goulart government through the federal literacy program which he directed. He does not espouse Marxist views in this work. His analysis of Brazilian society describes the gradual awakening of consciousness through which Brazil was passing, from naive consciousness of problems in society to a recognition of the need for modernizing efforts. He judges the failure of the governmental reforms to be due to the Brazilian people's lack of experience with democracy. The goal of the Goulart administration, and of Freire who worked within it, was not revolution but the democratization of the culture. Freire details reasons for the failure of this democratic experience, drawing heavily on the work of Gilberto Freyre, who described Brazilian society in terms of the relationships between masters and slaves.[2]

As described in an earlier chapter, Freire's religious vision comes through in this work in a number of ways. He tells us that the fullness of human existence is found in union with the Creator, a union that safeguards human freedom, which is the essential characteristic of humans. Freire speaks of human existence as a "dynamic concept, implying eternal dialogue between man and man, between man and the world, between man and his Creator. It is this dialogue which makes man an historical being."[3] Freire describes his position toward social change as a radical Christian position which is indebted to the thought of Emmanuel Mounier, a twentieth century French Christian philosopher. Freire, like other leftist Catholic intellectuals, drew heavily on the thought of Mounier, Teilhard de Chardin, and Jacques Maritain, in order to bring the Christian emphasis on personal freedom, social activism, and change to bear on modern problems and social movements. Freire quotes at length from Mounier's article on Christianity and the concept of progress. Freire also cites Pope John XXIII's encyclical letter "Christianity and Social Progress," which described the proper kind of relationship that should exist among individuals and among nations, a relationship of assistance without self-interest. This encyclical softened the Catholic Church's traditional condemnation of socialism by recognizing the need for socialization or social cooperation in and among nations.

The democratic society that Freire mapped out in *Education for Critical Consciousness* is clearly to be founded on Christian principles of freedom, justice, equality, and charity. Although references to Christian sources are not numerous in this work, they are significant. Freire states that persons' awareness of and living out of their relationship with the Creator is one of the important ingredients of that critical consciousness which is essential for the development of the new person and the new society. The kind of education that Freire proposes for bringing about his democratic society is described in religious terms borrowed from Karl Jaspers and Martin Buber, two religious existentialists who have influenced Freire's thinking. Educational dialogue for Freire is "nourished by love, humility, hope, faith, and trust. When the two poles of the dialogue are thus linked by love, hope, and mutual trust, they can join in a critical search for something."[4]

Some of the basic principles of a Christian social democratic philosophy are also found in *Pedagogy*. Freire addressed this book to both Christians and Marxists, even though he expected some disagreements from both groups. He was sensitive to the possibility that revolutionaries might tend to dismiss him because of certain concepts in his writings, notably those that come from his religious vision: ontological vocation, love, dialogue, hope, humility, and sympathy. Freire no doubt expected criticisms from some Christians for his adoption of many Marxist concepts, including the necessity for revolutionary violence. When Freire speaks of the necessity of violence or rebellion in this book, he describes these as acts of love. Freire also attributed the fatalism of oppressed groups to a false concept of God which, he contends, many of the oppressed have internalized. Freire also rejected the concept that the oppressors are the defenders of Western civilization.

What is new about *Pedagogy,* however, is that some elements of a Marxist critique have been introduced into Freire's social analysis, reflecting the radicalization that he underwent in the early years of his exile from Brazil. Freire now includes within his social theory an analysis of the class struggles that exist in developing countries. Yet the Marxist elements are connected to the principles that underlie his basically Christian view of society. Freire also maintains his belief in God as controlling history by directing the activity of humans. Furthermore, he maintains his basically religious view of the human person.

Increasingly in later writings and speeches, Freire states that the Christian gospel is a prophetic message in its call for the radical reordering of any society in which persons are oppressed. He appeals not only to the gospel but also to the social encyclicals of the popes. At a talk in Rome in 1970, he made these comments about his religious faith:

> I am not yet completely a Catholic. I just keep trying to be one more completely, day after day. . . . I just feel passionately, corporately, physically, with all my being, that my stance is a Christian one because it is 100 percent revolutionary and human and liberating, and hence committed and utopian.[5]

Freire's espousal of both the Christian and Marxist gospels is not surprising in light of developments with the Catholic Left in Latin American starting with the late 1950's. This Catholic Left, which had been nourished on the Christian humanism and Christian democracy of Mounier and Maritain, found itself working for social changes more and more with members of the Communist Party and committed Marxists. Consequently, many in the Catholic Left became increasingly interested in socialistic ideals. While attempting to maintain fundamental Christian belief, they embraced socialist concepts that had previously been rejected by church authorities. The "Base Document" drawn up by the Catholic Popular Action group in 1962 at the Dominican convent in Belo Horizonte is a manifestation of this attempt.[6] From a reading of the social teaching of the church, this document posited a historical movement leading toward socialization and a concept of persons as subjects and ends of this process. From Marxism it drew an emphasis on the importance of economic conditions, the inevitability of class struggle, a condemnation of imperialism, and the necessity of revolution for Latin American countries. In language that finds many parallels in Freire, Popular Action

> opted for a policy of revolutionary preparation, consisting of a mobilization of the people, on the basis of the development of their levels of consciousness and organization, securing this mobilization in a struggle against the double domination of capitalism (international and national) and feudalism.[7]

Freire's assimilation of Marxist ideas into a fundamentally Christian vision finds many parallels in other Latin American Christian thinkers. The various statements of the Latin American bishops conferences have utilized elements of a Marxist analysis of social, economic, and political situations existing in Latin American countries. These statements, however, have shied away from proposing socialist revolution as the necessary solution to these problems. Individual bishops, such as Helder Camara of Recife, Brazil, and Sergeo-Mendes of Cuernavaca, Mexico, did propose socialist solutions. Various groups of Christians, including priests, advocated the necessity of a socialist revolution along the lines of Cuba.[8]

Latin American Christians who have attempted to forge a marriage of the social teachings of Christianity and Marxism have opened themselves to criticism from more orthodox members in both groups. Orthodox Christians contend that Marxism is essentially contradictory to fundamental Christian faith because of its espousal of materialism, determinism, and atheism. For these Christians, a person embraces Marxism only at the expense of abandoning Christian faith. Many Marxists are equally convinced of the fundamental incompatibility of Marxism with any religion. Thus they reject the efforts of humanistic or revisionist Marxists as contrary to orthodox Marxist doctrine. It is upon these revisionists or neo-Marxists, such as Althusser, Kolakowsi, and Antonio Gramsci that Freire and other Latin American Christians draw.[9]

Freire recognizes that churches have traditionally been the centers of reaction and conservatism with regard to societal change, aligned as they have often been with the ruling classes. Yet he also recognizes that, "from the beginning of modern times, hopes for something new from God have emigrated from the Church and have been invested in revolution and rapid social change."[10] Freire is no doubt referring to the social teachings of popes and theologians as well as grass roots socio-religious movements.

ANALYSIS OF FREIRE'S SOCIAL THEORY

Freire's social theory begins with a criticism of Third World societies. He then attempts to apply these criticisms to other societies. In universalizing his analysis of Third World countries by using a general and almost metaphysical language, Freire has run the risk of providing a simplistic social analysis full of dichotomies: oppressors and oppressed, authentic and true liberation, open and closed societies, cultural invasion and cultural freedom, banking education and conscientization.

A point about Freire which is applicable to other areas of his thought might best be mentioned here. Freire's writings as well as his person are marked by a certain charismatic and prophetic quality. Prophets and charismatic persons are given to dramatic assertions, to putting things in black and white terms, to uttering condemnations of sin and evil, and to presenting idealized visions of a future. This trait may be another of the influences of religious culture on Freire. It is frustrating to bring cool analysis to this type of writing that eschews the nuances of academic language. Yet if the Freire theory is to remain influential in religious, social, and educational discourse, it must be subjected to a certain amount of criticism. Though true of all aspects of his thought, this is particularly important in discussions of his social theory, which contains his fundamental vision of the utopian society.

One of Freire's dichotomies is his division of societies into closed and open societies, with recognition being given to societies in the process of moving from closed to open. Closed and open societies become somewhat caricatured in his description. Drawing as he does on Freyre's analysis of the master-slave relationship, Freire tends to make draw too great a contrast between the two forms of societies. A closed society has many elements of openness that form the basis for the breaks that can develop in these societies. Also, societies never become completely open, despite the dream of utopian socialists. Freire, like other utopian thinkers, is constantly on the lookout for the society in which utopian dreams are being realized. Of course, he does not look to Russia. But he does at certain times hold up Mao's China, Castro's Cuba, and the Sandinista's Nicaragua. This search for a place where such dreams are realized is understandable, but it should be accompanied by more realism than Freire exhibits, as recent events have shown in China and Nicaragua.

In chapter four I pointed out some difficulties with Freire's use of the theme of oppression to analyze Third World countries. While this is an important concept, it has to be used in a more sophisticated manner than exhibited by Freire. The facile use of the dichotomy between oppressors and oppressed is too freely drawn. Freire recognizes that there is a process by which societies move from the state of large scale oppression to a realization that one must combat oppression actively. Yet oppression in society needs a more careful examination than he provides.

Freire singles out domination as a major theme in Third World countries. For him this is a condition that results from an unjust social order. The basic domination, in his view, comes from control of production by capitalists. For him this domination limits the consciousness of individuals with regard to their concrete situations. Nowhere, however, does he subject socialist systems to similar criticisms with regard to their tendencies to dominate the consciousness of their peoples and to develop into oppressive state socialisms. Freire directs his entire educational endeavor at combatting domination by fostering critical reflection in learners. He also describes this process as a social one. As pointed out in chapter four, however, Freire may be too sanguine about what people will do once they have arrived at a level of critical reflection. His failure to take into account the dark side of human nature leads him to neglect the possibilities that this critical reflection might be combined with self-interest to bring about a more oppressive situation than the previous system of domination.

As noted earlier, Freire now recognizes some of the weaknesses of his earlier analysis of society. He confesses that he did not sufficiently attend to the relationships between education and politics and neglected the problem of social classes and their struggle. He also recognizes that by omitting these essential elements he "opened the door to every sort of reactionary interpretation and practice, leading to many distortions of what conscientization must really be."[11] The concept of conscientization has been used in so many ways that Freire prefers not to use the term in more recent discussions.

Though Freire is a social and educational radical, he does accept many of the principles of liberal social thought. Because of his emphasis on human freedom in the knowing process, Freire, like many liberals, notably John Dewey, locates authority not in past traditions but within the individual. History and the cultural past are for him institutions that persons should attempt to transcend and leave behind. Though this may be true in some cultural situations, this negative attitude towards history and tradition elevated to the level of general theory, bespeaks a lack of awareness of how important traditions, culture, and the past are in human life and knowing. Freire's method of critical reflection which places the source of authority within the individual may dangerously lead to the relativization of all traditions, histories, and values. As will be seen in a later chapter, this may be the most serious objection to the use of conscientization as a theological method.

Freire's acceptance of participatory democracy as the preferred form of government is another manifestation of his liberal thought. This is a very Western idea and does not appear to allow openness to other forms of democracy, let alone other forms of government. One does not find in Freire a discussion of the checks and balances which are needed for democracy to preserve the rights of all individuals.

If one turns to recent "spoken books" of Freire, one finds that Freire is aware of criticisms of this type as well as other criticisms to be made in this book. Yet the Freire theory that has had influence and will continue to have influence is that found in his major works written early in his career. No doubt *Pedagogy* will take its place among educational classics, much as Dewey's *Democracy and Education* represents the classic statement of progressive education, notwithstanding efforts of both authors to qualify and modify these works by later statements.

FREIRE'S CRITIQUE OF THE CHURCHES

Most of Freire's social criticism is directed at political and economic systems. The one institution of society that he subjects to his radical social criticisms is the church, meaning especially the Catholic Church in Latin America. His criticisms of the social policies of churches thus gives a concreteness to his general social criticisms and also provides some insights into his theological concepts.

In 1970 Freire became an educational consultant with the World Council of Churches in Geneva. When he was in this position, he began to direct more of his attention to theology and to a criticism of institutional religion. This criticism takes a rather general form and is not usually long on references to particular countries or problems. Freire's social analysis of religious institutions is important, for the churches play a major role in many countries of the Third World.

In "The Educational Role of the Churches in Latin America" Freire criticized the churches for failing to exercise the true prophetic function which is theirs.[12] He urged the churches to work actively against oppression in whatever form it is found. The churches, in his view, cannot be neutral with regard to various oppressions in society, because neutrality implies supporting the *status quo*. Examples of oppressions include class determined societies, oppressive power elites, and capitalism. The true Christian gospel in his view should be prophetic, utopian, and revolutionary in calling for believers to work for change, revolution, and liberation. Jesus is depicted by Freire as a person who worked for radical change. The religious revolutionary is involved in living out the Passover or Easter through denouncing oppression and announcing liberation. Redemption is interpreted as the Christian's willingness to undergo death by struggling for new life and freedom for oppressed people.

Freire contends that for the churches to respond to the gospel they must be truly prophetic and revolutionary. He argues that the churches must dare to take sides in struggles for political liberation, otherwise they will actually end up supporting repressive regimes. He charges churches with excessive involvement in bureaucractic paper shuffling, of "dying of cold in the warm bosom of the bourgeoisies."[13]

Freire's discussion of the religious person's participation in revolution seems to include an approval of the use of violent means to achieve revolutionary purposes. He speaks approvingly of those Christians who "recognize revolution as the road to liberation for the oppressed classes, and the military coup as a revolutionary option." He adds:

> Today's Latin American Christians . . . will disagree at times, especially over the proper tactics to be used, but there are those who . . . commit themselves to the oppressed classes and stay firm in that position. . . . These individuals, some churchmen and some laymen, had to take their bruises and cuts during the transition so as to move on from an idealistic view of reality to a dialectical one.[13]

It is easy to understand how Freire came to the controversial view, especially in pacifist religious circles, that violence may at times be justified in the struggle against oppression. He had experienced what he considered the detrimental effects of nonintervention of the Latin American churches in the struggles of oppressed peoples to achieve authentic liberation. In these instances nonintervention was, for Freire, siding with the oppressors. Also, Freire is an activist who has always been involved in political struggles. Che Guevara and Camilo Torres appear in his works as revolutionary heroes.

In his criticism of the churches Freire echoes Latin American theologians of liberation who have been so critical of traditional church structures and policies that they have come into conflict with Vatican authorities. This theology of liberation is in some ways similar to the social gospel that developed in the United States in the late nineteenth century as a challenge to traditional churches and in response to the general shock of urbanization and industrialization. The master motif of the social gospel was the coming of the Kingdom of God through the progressive growth of love in society. It emphasized social and political action and attempted to combat subjectivism, otherworldliness and false apocalypticism in religion. Harvey Cox reintroduced a form of this social gospel into the theological world in the 1960's by challenging the churches to join secular movements.[15] For Cox such involvements constituted the essential mission of the churches. In a more recent work Cox judges the liberation theology emphasis as a major development in developing a postmodern Christianity.[16]

Fundamental to this type of theology is a particular concept of God. The symbol of God presented in this theology is not the Unmoved Mover of Aristotle or the Subsistent Being of Thomas Aquinas. It is rather the active and dynamic God of the Hebrews and the humanity of Jesus. For liberation theologians God is someone who acts to save humankind from oppression and domination. God is forever creating men and women and the world with their cooperation. God delivers a people from bondage. Jesus is the radical critic of oppressive institutions. In this view, the symbol of God as savior refers not so much to individual salvation but the painful process of bringing people and societies to true freedom. The main task of the Christian is not to save his or her soul but to work with God in saving the world by combating all forms of human oppression. Original sin is given a social interpretation as referring to all forces of evil which humans and God struggle against and which prevent true freedom. The resurrection and future life with God are concrete symbols of the new life that exists in a utopian future.

This interpretation of the God symbol is operative in Freire's social criticism. In his earliest work, *Education for Critical Consciousness,* he presented God as a person who stands not for the domination of humans but for their liberation. He contends that "man's transcendent relationship is one in which man's freedom is guaranteed."[17] In *Pedagogy* he attacked what he considered the false view of God that fosters fatalism in oppressed peoples.[18] This distortion is based on the myth that rebellion is a sin against God. In "A letter to a Theology Student" Freire described the dynamic nature of the God symbol underlying his social criticism:

> The Word of God is inviting me to re-create the world, not for my brothers' domination but for their liberation. . . . The Word of God is not some content to be poured into us as if we were mere static recipients for it. And because it [the Word of God] saves, that Word also liberates, but men have to accept it historically. They must make themselves subjects, agents of their salvation.[19]

In this letter, Freire relates his work explicitly to the theology of liberation or utopian theology of some Latin Americans:

> Theology has to take its starting point from anthropology. That is why I insist that a utopian and prophetic theology leads naturally to a cultural action for liberation, and hence to conscientization.[20]

This utopian and prophetic theology, according to Freire, should begin with a new notion of God as "a presence in history, [who] does not in the slightest keep man from making history—the history of his liberation."[21]

In concluding this section, it should be noted that Freire directed his attention in a special manner to a criticism of education and social structures in Third World countries. Since his educational criticism will be treated at length in a later chapter, I merely want to note it at this point. This criticism also has a religious basis. Freire clearly sees a connection between theology, liberation, and education. Freire made this connection clearly in an interview when he responded:

How must my attitude be, for example, before the Word of God? I think that my attitude cannot be the attitude of an empty being waiting to be filled by the Word of God. I think also that in order to listen to it, it is necessary to be engaged in the process of the liberation of man. Because of this, I think that theology, such a theology, should be connected with education for liberation—and education for liberation with theology.[22]

One sees here a religious basis for Freire's criticism of what he calls "banking education." Just as God does not educate us by pouring the word into us, so we should not educate by merely pouring or depositing ready made knowledge into the minds of students. Human words, just like divine, have the power to liberate individuals.

Since returning to Latin America, Freire has had contacts with basic Christian communities. He is much impressed with the teachings of the churches and the analysis of some theologians. He speaks in glowing terms of his contacts with the more prophetic elements of the church in Brazil and Latin America.

ANALYSIS OF FREIRE'S CRITIQUE OF CHURCHES IN LATIN AMERICA

Keeping with his prophetic stance and mode of speaking, Freire's analysis of three different types of churches in Latin America makes a great deal of sense. Yet there are the usual exaggerations and distortions when his words are examined more carefully. In his severe criticism of the traditionalist church he fails to recognize the importance of tradition for religion and churches. An essential task of churches is to bring the past traditions to bear. In his judgment the efforts of these churches are alienating and paralyzing. For many involved in these churches they provide a support and a meaning. There is no doubt much to criticize in popular religion and in traditionalist churches; but this does not mean that people are necessarily not reaching humanization through the efforts of these churches.

Freire utters equally harsh judgments on churches that are only attempting to modernize. If he truly realized the power of traditions and history in churches, he would applaud these efforts rather than judge them severely from the standpoint of a utopian religious consciousness. If he realized the great struggles between those who attempt to conserve a tradition, however lifeless it may have become, and those who attempt to renew it by adopting more contemporary modes of religious life, he would have more sympathy for the reformers and modernizers. It is interesting that Freire has a similar lack of understanding for reformist elements in the churches as his radical critics had for his reformist efforts in Brazil and Chile when he actually worked within the governments to bring about reform. His efforts in aiding African countries in the literacy projects were also reformist in nature.

Freire's words on the prophetic churches do present an ideal for churches in Latin America and elsewhere. Freire seems to sense the unreality of his remarks when he states that the "prophetic perspective does not represent an escape into a world of unattainable dreams. It demands a scientific knowledge of the world as it really is."[23] Freire is prophetic here in describing the utopian church, which he finds in the basic Christian communities of Brazil and other Latin American countries. These communities are truly significant but neither they, nor any churches, fully live up to his utopian dreams. A closer look at the communities reveals that they have many of the same problems that afflict all organizations and associations. This is not to deny the spiritual vitality of these communities. For many they are the wave of the future. Yet their own makeup and future is still rather debatable.

In summary then, a number of criticisms have been made of Freire's social theory. At times his theory is vague, general, and imprecise. Freire rarely presents evidence of an empirical nature or cites sociological research for his analysis. He is also too prone to divide societies into good and bad without offering adequate criteria by which this distinction is made. Freire's analysis of Brazilian society appears inadequate, when compared to other analyses made by social scientists. In his analysis of the role of the churches in Latin American countries, he does not indicate how the churches are both part of the problem and part of the solution to the problem.

NOTES

1. Emmanuel de Kadt. *Catholic Radicals in Brazil*. London: Oxford University Press, 1970.

2. Gilberto Freyre. *The Masters and the Slaves.* New York: Knopf, 1964.
3. Paulo Freire. *Education for Critical Consciousness.* New York; Continuum, 1973, p. 18.
4. Paulo Freire. *Education for Critical Consciousness,* p. 45.
5. Paulo Freire, cited in John W. Donohoe. "Paulo Freire— Philosopher of Adult Education." *America,* Vol. CXXVII, No. 7, 1972, p. 170.
6. Thomas G. Sanders. "Brazil: A Catholic Left." *America,* Vol. CXVII, 1967, pp. 598–601.
7. Thomas G. Sanders. "Brazil: A Catholic Left," p. 600.
8. *First Encounter of Christians for Socialism: The Final Document.* Washington, D.C.: LADOC, 3, 8a, 1973.
9. Louis Althusser. *For Marx.* New York: Random House, 1970; Leszek Kolakowski. *Towards a Marxist Humanism.* New York: Grove Press, 1968; Antonio Gramsci. *Cultura y literature.* Madrid: Ediciones Peninsula, 1967.
10. Paulo Freire. *The Politics of Education.* South Hadley: Mass.: Bergin and Garvey, 1985, p. 141.
11. Paulo Freire. *The Politics of Education,* p. 152.
12. Paulo Freire. "The Educational Role of the Churches in Latin America." Washington, D.C.: LADOC, 2, 29c, 1972.
13. Paulo Freire. "The Educational Role of the Churches in Latin America," p. 9.
14. Paulo Freire. "The Educational role of the Churches in Latin America," p. 12.
15. Harvey Cox. *The Secular City.* New York: Macmillan, 1965.
16. Harvey Cox. *Religion in the Secular City.* New York: Simon and Schuster, 1984.
17. Paulo Freire. *La Educacion como practica de la libertad,* Santiago, Chile: ICIRA, Calle Arturo Caro, 1969, p. 15.
18. Paulo Freire. *Pedagogy of the Oppressed,* New York: Continuum, 1970, p. 162.
19. Paulo Freire. "A Letter to a Theology Student. *Catholic Mind,* Vol. LXX, No. 1265, 1972, p. 7.
20. Paulo Freire. "A Letter to a Theology Student," p. 8.
21. Paulo Freire. "A Letter to a Theology Student," p. 8.
22. Paulo Freire. "Education for Awareness: Talk with Paulo Freire." *Risk,* Vol. VI, No. 4, 1970, p. 17).
23. Paulo Freire. *The Politics of Education,* p. 138.

CHAPTER 7

Revolutionary Theory and Strategy

Freire has achieved the reputation of being a revolutionary educator. His *Pedagogy of the Oppressed* has been called a handbook for revolutionary education. The revolution he proposes is both political and cultural, intended to bring about a radical restructuring of societies in the Third World. Although Freire's emphasis is on political revolution, he proposes a liberating education as a necessity for bringing about this revolution. *Pedagogy* describes the type of revolution that must take place in order to initiate a revolution among oppressed peoples. Within Freire's proposals for political revolution there are discussions that touch on his religious vision.

Though Freire at times couches his political and educational theory in general terms, it is important to recall that his political views were developed in countries which may be termed prerevolutionary or open to dramatic changes in government. His literacy work in Brazil was part of a reformist political administration that ran afoul of entrenched economic powers. In Chile he aided the agricultural reform efforts of the Christian Democratic government. In more recent years he has consulted with socialist and Marxist governments in Africa and Nicaragua, aiding them in developing an education that would be both liberating and contributory to economic growth. Freire relates his ideas less easily to the political systems of western democracies and has rarely mentioned countries in Eastern Europe.

THE REVOLUTIONARY EDUCATOR

Freire's revolutionary politics spring mainly from his political and educational experiences in Brazil. His position was not revolutionary in the beginning but became so after the failed efforts of the Goulart government to democratize the Brazilian masses. Freire's involvement with reformist politics has been a point of criticism directed against him by those who know him only as the political revolutionary. On a number of occasions in interviews, he has responded to these criticisms by pointing to the fact that his educational and political efforts were viewed as revolutionary in the context of Brazil in the early 1960's.

Although Freire has the reputation of being a revolutionary educator and has penned a classic manual on this type of education, he makes it clear that he himself has never participated in the type of revolutionary activity that he propounded in *Pedagogy:*

> It is possible that some may question my right to discuss revolutionary action, a subject of which I have no concrete experience. However, the fact that I have not personally participated in revolutionary action does not negate the possibility of my reflecting on this theme.[1]

Freire contends that in his experience as an educator, he has "accumulated a comparative wealth of material which challenged [him] to run the risk of making the affirmations contained in this work."[2] Of course, for years he was involved as a lawyer and educator in efforts to bring about changes in Brazil. Yet when compared with revolutionary efforts needed to bring down a government and put another in its place, one can question his lack of concrete experience. More recently, Freire has gathered more information about revolutionary politics through his work with new nations and new governments in the Third World.

The sense in which Freire's pedagogy may be considered revolutionary was explained by the Brazilian sociologist Francisco Weffort in his introduction to the Brazilian edition of *Education for Critical Consciousness*. Freire's goals of literacy for the Brazilian masses and increased popular political participation as a member of the Federal Ministry of Education were part of attempts of the Goulart government to democratize the Brazilian culture. His work was certainly viewed as revolutionary by certain right wing groups. Weffort describes how Freire's work might be considered revolutionary:

> If education for freedom [Freire's literacy campaign] carried the seed of revolt, it would not be correct to say that this is one of the educator's objectives. If it occurs, it is only and exclusively because conscientization discerns a reality in which guidance and conflict are the most frequent data.[3]

Weffort criticized the Popular Culture Movement, of which Freire was a part, for its failure to be more political. He contends that the "forces interested in popular mobilization failed to perceive and exploit the implications that conscientization had for action."[4] He admits that the popular movements had political relevance. Their inability, however, to be truly effective politically resulted from the fact that these movements were "committed directly or indirectly to the government and thus to the existing institutions which were themselves the objects of popular pressure."[5] The Popular Culture Movement failed, in his view, because of an overinvestment in education at the expense of concrete political goals and strategies. Weffort also suggests that reformers like Freire were prevented from bringing about necessary changes for the masses because of the state support they received.[6] They were in this way compromised by conflicting loyalties. It is clear from later comments of Freire that he basically agrees with this assessment, for he terms his political views at this time as naive.

In reading of *Educacao*, a work written immediately after Freire's exile from Brazil and begun while he was in jail, one comes up with no evidence of a revolutionary thrust. While working in Brazil at this time, he desired only to bring about gradual changes through his educational efforts. The purpose of his educational practice was to make the people aware of themselves as reflective human beings who were capable of creating both history and culture. His literacy campaign was promoted by the Goulart government for at least one political purpose—the enfranchisement of the masses, who would then support the government in the upcoming elections.

In *Pedagogy* Freire explicitly turned his attention to education as a means for bringing about a revolution. Reasons for this conversion have been given earlier in this book. As I have indicated, *Pedagogy* is not based on actual experience in revolutionary movements. This explains the disillusionment that many political radicals have experienced in reading Freire's works or in attending training sessions which he conducts. People expect an active revolutionary but they meet "another religious, middle-class reformer."[7] Egerton, at a conference in South Carolina in 1973, pointedly summed up this criticism of Freire:

> Freire is no more radical than most of us. There is no originality in what he says—it's the same old rap. He has lectured us, criticized our narrow focus on small problems, but his alternative—the global perspective—is stale rhetoric. He is a political and ideological theoretician, not an educator. There is nothing concrete and specific in what he says.[8]

Freire, the revolutionary educator, advised public school teachers at this conference to work within the system and to be satisfied with doing the little that they could do there. He also admonished them to do the great many things they can do outside the system.

Helpful or not, this type of criticism sharpens the focus on the nature of the revolutionary education advocated by Freire. He does not propose it for all situations. He certainly did suggest it for some Latin American countries in the 1970's. Freire has never been comfortable addressing North American audiences, for he is aware of the great differences between Third World and First World countries. When brought into discussions about school systems in North America, there is little that he is able to recommend except some form of liberating education, which is decidedly reformist.[9]

RELIGIOUS JUSTIFICATION OF REVOLUTION

In *Pedagogy* and other works Freire presented a theory of revolutionary education for some countries in the Third World. In doing this he has been sensitive to the question of whether or not political revolution, especially violent revolution, can be justified according to Christian principles. The religious inspiration of revolution has been discussed by a number of scholars.[10] This question, which has long been discussed, especially in Catholic leftist circles in Latin America, is an issue that has brought radical Catholics into conflict with church hierarchies in Latin American countries.

Latin American Christians can be divided into four main categories with regard to their attitudes toward revolution in society. One group, which includes many traditional Catholics, denies the need for changes in the existing social and political systems. A second group sees the need for some change but does not think that the church as an institution should be involved in directly working for these changes, for they view this task as the responsibility of lay persons. A third group views change as necessary and believes that the church should directly participate in this change. This is the attitude of many lay persons engaged in politics, and the attitude of the Catholic Bishops at their conference in Medellin in 1968. There is some debate whether priests and members of religious communities of sisters and brothers should engage in political activity. Church authorities in Rome have definitely prohibited this type of activity in Latin America and other parts of the world. Finally, there is a fourth category of Latin American Christians who believe that only violent revolution can effectively change the situation in some countries where massive oppression leads to a denial of basic human rights. These Christians have committed themselves to the revolutionary process and have collaborated with various Marxist movements. In recent years a small number of clergy and theologians have joined the ranks of this group.[11]

By 1970 Freire definitely put himself into league with the latter group of Christians. In speaking of the myths which the oppressor society has imposed upon the oppressed, he points to two in particular that bear on this issue: "The myth of the heroism of the oppressor classes as defenders of Western civilization . . .; the myth that rebellion is a sin against God."[12] The implication here, which is supported by other writings, is that Freire sees rebellion and revolution as acts that can be in accord with Christian and religious principles. Freire goes on to describe revolutionary violence in terms that have clear religious connotations:

> I am more and more convinced that true revolutionaries must perceive the revolution, because of its creative and liberating nature, as an act of love. For me, the revolution which is impossible without a theory of revolution—and therefore science—is not irreconcilable with love.[13]

In later writings Freire becomes more explicit in his justification of Christian participation in revolutionary action. In his "Letter to a Theology Student," he asserted:

> We, as Christians, have an enormous task to perform, presuming that we are capable of setting aside our idealistic myths and in that way sharing in the revolutionary transformation of society, instead of stubbornly denying the important contribution of Karl Marx.[14]

He also affirms in the letter that the Word of God demands a willingness to work for human liberation through a process that entails challenging the powerful of the earth.[15]

Freire's most outspoken statement on religious justification for revolutionary action is found in his article, "The Educational Role of the Churches in Latin America."[16] The church, he contends, cannot remain neutral toward political activity. It must work for the radical transformation of social structures. He criticizes conservatives in the churches for "castrating the church's prophetic dimension and fearing the radical transformation of the unjust world."[17] He praises the developing political theology of liberation which dares to say something about the revolutionary transformation of the world. Within this prophetic theology there is room, he avers, for the bold stance of "revolution as the road to liberation for the oppressed classes, and the military coup as a revolutionary option."[18] He admits that there may be differences over tactics among Christians dedicated to revolutionary action, but he commends the firm commitment of these Christians.

Freire, on a number of occasions, uses two religious metaphors in urging Christians to become involved in revolutionary activity: Passover and Easter. Both of these liberating events entailed struggles of life and death. These deeply religious acts of redemption and liberation from oppression were achieved through active resistance and violent death. Thus, according to Freire, Christians who participate in revolutionary action against oppression take part in a new Passover, a new Easter. The revolutionaries' "setting out is really a sort of Passover in which they will have to die as an oppressed class, in order to be reborn as a class that liberates itself."[19] Freire also envisions the prophetic church which does not allow itself to be made a refuge for the oppressed masses, but rather invites them to a new Exodus.

Another powerful example that Freire uses in urging Latin American Christians into revolutionary action is Jesus. The image of Christ he presents is that of a radical, not satisfied with the *status quo*, anxious to move on, and one who is willing to die in order to bring about a continuous rebirth. Freire puts these words in the mouth of those who would counsel a conservative activity on the part of Christians: "They say to Christ: 'Master, why push on, if everything here is so beautiful?' "[20]

Another interesting development surfaces in the writings of Freire. He has clearly become an advocate of revolutionary action for oppressed peoples in the Third World. This change, however, has been accompanied by a change from a less explicit religious justification of revolution to a more explicit legitimation of Christian participation in revolutionary activity. The failure to become involved in this type of action in certain countries in Latin America is a failure to live up to the Gospel.

Freire's open advocacy of revolution on religious principles resonates with Latin American theologians with whom Freire is familiar. He expressed his desire to meet with theologians who proposed a political theology of liberation. Freire's position on the religious justification for revolution is similar to that of Gustavo Gutierrez, one of Latin America's leading Christian theologians, who has attempted to give religious justification for the more revolutionary political postures of Christian groups in Latin America. He appeals to the message of the gospel:

> What ultimately brings Christians to participate in liberating oppressed peoples is the conviction that the gospel message is radically incompatible with an unjust society. They see clearly that they cannot be authentic Christians unless they act.[21]

Gutierrez discusses revolution in the context of the biblical symbols of creation and salvation as well as the prophetic promises for a kingdom of peace. He makes the case for active church involvement in revolution in these terms:

> In Latin America, the church must realize that it exists in a continent undergoing revolution, where violence is present in different ways. The world in which the Christian community is called to live . . . is one in social revolution. Its mission must be achieved keeping that in account. The church has no alternative. Only a total break with the unjust order to which it is bound in a thousand conscious or unconscious ways, and a forthright commitment to a new society, will make men in Latin America believe the message of love it bears.[22]

Freire has praise for Christians who have espoused the revolutionary cause. In a number of places in his writings, he makes reference to the example of Camilo Torres, the Colombian priest-sociologist who became involved in politics and was ultimately killed as a guerilla. Torres, in his serious attempt to articulate a theory of liberation consonant with orthodox Christian values, stated that Catholics in Columbia had a moral responsibility to participate in the revolution. Freire admired the commitment of Torres to the people—as a priest, as a Christian, and as a revolutionary. Torres is referred to as the guerrilla priest and a loving man.[23]

THEORY AND STRATEGY OF REVOLUTION

It has already been pointed out that Freire has had no direct involvement with revolutionary activity. He indicates that he has gained insights into this activity from his educational experiences in Brazil and Chile. His theory of revolution draws on a number of sources. He cites the writings of Mao Tse-Tung, Herbert Marcuse, Franz Fanon, Regis Debray, Che Guevara, Karl Marx, Nicolai Lenin, Fidel Castro, and others.

Freire's theory of political revolution is based on themes articulated in *Pedagogy*. Freire does what he promised here; he brings educational themes to bear on the forging of a revolution. He notes that the oppressed, once freed, will go through a stage of sub-oppressors since they do not have a consciousness of themselves as an oppressed class. He argues that a knowledge of causes of oppression is essential for both leaders and people, highlighting the necessity for education. The oppressed must see oppression as a limit situation they can overcome. Revolution must include dialogue and communion with the oppressed at all stages. It is necessary for the dominating class to disappear, even if this means the use of violence. Freire recognizes that some members of the oppressor class may be able to join the oppressed, after committing class suicide. The total revolution should include cultural revolution, the conscientization of all through establishing permanent dialogue in society, and the necessity for organizing the leaders with the people.

Freire's theory and strategy of revolution, as expressed in *Pedagogy*, appear to be rather naive. For the most part, he discusses revolution without analyzing any particular social and historical contexts. Generalizing from his reflections upon the Brazilian situation in which he was involved, he is like the crusader who, after the brave and good fight, stands ready to generalize his theories and strategies to the situation of all oppressed peoples. His simplistic analysis of Brazilian society into the oppressors and the oppressed in *Pedagogy* does not do justice even to that historical situation, let alone provide the basis for making generalizations.

The most serious problem with his discussion of revolution is that by attempting to bring educational concerns to the forefront in revolutionary action, he almost reduces a political revolution to an educational enterprise. Little attention is given to concrete political realities. In discussing such revolutionaries as Castro and Guevara, he concentrates on bringing them into line with his concepts of communion and dialogue with the people, without criticizing them for their antidialogic tactics.

Although *Pedagogy* does not give an analysis of concrete historical and social situations, in other places he does provide this dimension for prerevolutionary Brazil of the early 1960's.[24] The situation was one in which there were only two possibilities: a coup d'etat or a revolution. The coup d'etat was the answer of the military and industrial elites to movements for democratic participation. When Freire describes the revolutionary leadership needed for this situation, his recommendations become highly intellectual. For example, revolutionary leadership must know reality, proclaim a new reality, rely on the people and objective facts as their source of knowledge, act in communion with the people.

A fundamental flaw in Freire's theory of revolution is his inadequate treatment of "oppression." For Freire, "any situation in which A objectively exploits B or hinders his pursuit of self-affirmation as a responsible person is one of oppression."[25] Further, he describes an action as oppressive when "it interferes with man's ontological vocation to be more fully human."[26] For Freire, the goal of liberation from oppression is the humanization of persons. Oppression is always an act of violence since it treats persons as if they were things.

The problem of oppression, for Freire, is reduced to the problem of dehumanization. Freire appears to carry with him some intuitive concept of what it means to be human. He tries to defend himself against the charges of idealism and subjectivism in his philosophy, yet he admits some "naive" expressions in his writings that give credence to these charges. However, without spelling out his criteria for self-affirmation or humanization of the person, his description of oppression becomes not only abstract but also dangerous. Unless one sets down objective criteria for exploitation, determining what is oppressive becomes the judgment of each individual and group. Freire would certainly not affirm this. He is convinced that through his pedagogy the oppressed with their leaders will come to intuit reality the way it is. Freire's doctrine of objective exploitation comes dangerously close to the concept of the objective enemy which Hannah Arendt criticized:

> The chief difference between the despotic and the totalitarian secret police lies in the difference between the "suspect" and "the objective enemy." The latter is defined by the policy of the government and not by his own desire to overthrow it.[27]

Freire describes only one relationship in the Third World, the relationship of oppression and subjection. Certainly a number of other relationships exist there. Even with regard to more advanced technological countries Freire thinks only in terms of oppressor-oppressed relationships. The oppressors in these societies are those who use technology to manipulate people and to produce a mass society. Freire does not condemn technology in itself, but rather its harmful effects. The treatment that Freire gives to technology is not extensive. When he does discuss humans and technology, he relies on his usual theoretical framework—dependence, subjection, and oppression.[28]

The tendency of Freire to see only one type of relationship among persons makes it difficult to apply his pedagogy of revolution. The cultural, social, political, and religious are not differentiated in his work. It is easy for Freire to do this in *Pedagogy* because he fails to root his revolutionary theory in any particular historical or cultural context. In attempting to forge a universal theory of revolutionary pedagogy, he oversimplifies to a dangerous degree the concept of oppression and his pedagogical program. He appears to be unaware in this work that revolutions differ according to particular social and economic situations. Freire's failure to link his revolutionary theory to a particular historical situation makes his theory rather abstract, and separates him from such theorists as Johnson and Arendt, who consider these contexts essential in defining revolution.[29] This leaning towards abstraction also renders his theory of revolution almost impossible to apply.

Freire considers his emphasis on the "dialogical nature" of revolutionary action to be his main contribution to a theory of revolution. He believes that leaders should be in constant dialogue with the people at all points in the revolution. In fact, he points to his experience in "dialogical" and problem solving education as giving him the necessary experience to write a book on revolutionary action. *Pedagogy* was written to defend the eminently pedagogical character of the revolution. Freire contends that:

> Critical and liberating dialogue, which presupposes action, must be carried on with the oppressed at whatever the stage of their struggle for liberation. The content of that dialogue can and should vary in accordance with historical conditions and the level at which they can perceive reality.[30]

Freire's commitment to the dialogical character of the revolution is a rather limited one, as appears from his writings. After he indicates the number of cases where dialogue among equals is to be suspended, there is little left to his theory about the dialogical nature of the revolution. Freire has great difficulty in making his hero, Che Guevara, an advocate of dialogical revolutionary action. He quotes the revolutionary leader's words:

> Mistrust: at the beginning, do not trust your own shadow; never trust friendly peasants, informers, guides, or contact men. Do not trust anything or anybody until a zone is completely liberated.[31]

Guevara does advocate communion with the people after liberation has been achieved. This, however, does not, as Freire would wish it to do, make Guevara an advocate of dialogue with the people at every stage of the revolution. Although Freire commends the realism of the guerrilla leader, he still attempts to make him an example of one who practiced his theory of revolutionary dialogue. But this appears impossible. In commending Guevara's mistrust of the ambiguity of oppressed men and women and his refusal to dialogue with them, Freire has denied the very heart of his theory of revolutionary action as fundamentally dialogical.

Freire compromises his dialogical theory of revolution in a number of other instances. He denies the revolutionaries' need to dialogue with the former oppressors. He agrees with Guevara's admonition to punish the deserter from the revolutionary action for the purpose of preserving cohesion and discipline in the group. Freire agrees with the guerilla leader in his nontolerance of those who are not ready to accept the conclusion that revolution is essential. He speaks of the revolution as loving and creating life: "And in order to create life, it [the revolution] may be obliged to prevent some men from circumscribing life."[32]

In *Pedagogy* Freire valiantly tries to shore up his theory of the dialogical character of the revolution against the stated views of revolutionaries. The effort, however, must be pronounced a failure. The forging of a revolution would seem to preclude any dialogue among equals to arrive at truth by permitting the free expression of ideas, as the revolutionary theorist Debray has noted.[33] Freire, the educator without experience in revolutionary action, has exaggerated the role that the free educational process is able to play in forging a revolution.

This exaggeration stems from a more fundamental problem: his inadequate treatment of education through dialogue. Briefly put, Freire believes that through dialogue people will somehow come to see objective reality. In this process, they will denounce what is truly oppressive and, at the same time, announce or proclaim a new nonoppressive reality. In announcing this new reality, they are already engaged in the process of working for its concrete realization. Freire is convinced that total freedom must be ensured to people involved in such dialogical education. It is Freire's philosophical position that an objective reality exists, which all will inevitably come to recognize through education. This almost quixotic view fails, however, to do justice to the complex nature of reality and of human knowledge of it. It leaves little room for a relativism and a pluralism of world views.

Freire is also rather vague in his description of the process and strategy of revolution, as many writers on revolutionary theory are. Revolutionary leadership for him will usually be made up of persons who have belonged in one way or another to the social class of the dominators in society. Inauthentic leaders will be made manifest through the practice of the dialectic. The leaders are able to organize themselves with the people. Freire admits that he has no details on how the revolution is to take place:

Instead of following predetermined plans, leaders and people, mutually identified, together create the guidelines of their action. In this synthesis, leaders and people are somehow reborn in new knowledge and new action.[34]

CONCLUSION

It appears that the weakest part of Freire's theory is his theory of political revolution. This is somewhat understandable since it is the activity with which he has had the least direct involvement. In later writings he has discussed details of revolutionary action, especially Marxist theory, at a highly abstract and theoretical level.

NOTES

1. Paulo Freire. *Pedagogy of the Oppressed.* New York: Continuum, 1970, p. 24.
2. Paulo Freire. *Pedagogy,* p. 24.
3. Francisco Weffort. "Education and Politics." Introduction to Paulo Freire, *Educacao como pratica da libertade.* Cambridge, Mass.: Center for the Study of Development and Social Change, 1969, p. 11.
4. Francisco Weffort. "Education and Politics," p. 11.
5. Francisco Weffort. "Education and Politics," p. 9.
6. Francisco Weffort. "Education and Politics," p. 29.
7. John Egerton. "Searching for Freire." *Saturday Review of Education,* Vol. 1, No. 3, 1973, p. 34.
8. John Egerton. "Searching for Freire," p. 35.
9. Ira Shor and Paulo Freire. *A Pedagogy for Liberation.* South Hadley, Mass.: Bergin and Harvey, 1987.
10. Hanna Arendt. *On Revolution.* New York: Viking Press, 1963; Crane Brinton. *The Anatomy of Revolution.* New York: Random House, 1965.
11. Francois Houtart and Antoine Rousseau. *The Church and Revolution.* New York: Orbis Books, 1971.
12. Paulo Freire. *Pedagogy,* pp. 136–137.
13. Paulo Freire. *Pedagogy,* p. 77.

14. Paulo Freire. "A Letter to a Theology Student." *Catholic Mind,* Vol. LXX, No. 1265, 1972, p. 7.
15. Paulo Freire. "A Letter to a Theology Student," p. 7.
16. Paulo Freire. "The Educational Role of the Churches in Latin America." Washington, D.C.: LADOC, 3, 14, 1972.
17. Paulo Freire. "The Educational Role of the Churches in Latin America," p. 3.
18. Paulo Freire. "The Educational Role of the Churches in Latin America," p. 12.
19. Paulo Freire. "The Educational Role of the Churches in Latin America," p. 4.
20. Paulo Freire. "The Educational Role of the Churches in Latin America," p. 12.
21. Gustavo Gutierrez. *A Theology of Liberation.* New York: Orbis, 1973, p. 72.
22. Gustavo Gutierrez. *A Theology of Liberation,* pp. 76–77.
23. Paulo Freire. *Pedagogy,* pp. 162, 171.
24. Paulo Freire. *Cultural Action for Freedom.* Cambridge, Mass.: *Harvard Educational Review* and Center for the Study of Development and Social Change, 1970; *The Politics of Education,* pp. 80–81.
25. Paulo Freire. *Pedagogy,* p. 40.
26. Paulo Freire. *Pedagogy,* pp. 40–41.
27. Hannah Arendt. *The Origins of Totalitarianism.* New York: Meridien Books, 1967, p. 423.
28. Paulo Freire. *Pedagogy,* pp. 49–50.
29. Chambers Johnson. *Revolutionary Change.* Boston: Little, Brown and Co., 1966; Hannah Arendt. *On Revolution.*
30. Paulo Freire. *Pedagogy,* p. 52.
31. Che Guevara cited in Freire. *Pedagogy,* p. 169.
32. Paulo Freire. *Pedagogy,* p. 171.
33. Regis Debray. *Revolution in the Revolution.* New York: Grove Press, 1967, pp. 56, 111.
34. Paulo Freire. *Pedagogy,* p. 183.

CHAPTER 8

Radical Critic of Banking Education

Paulo Freire is regarded as the originator of a revolutionary pedagogy which has relevance to education in many areas. He has also become noted for his criticisms of educational theory and practice both in Third World and First World countries. Many of his criticisms are centered on the methods used in traditional literacy education. He groups his criticisms around an attack on the banking approach to education.

Freire's educational criticism has had an impact in many fields of education. Literacy educators have found his ideas a challenge to the traditional methods of teaching adults basic reading and writing skills. Adult educators in many fields have also found in his writings a summons not only to reexamine their methods but also to question their understanding of the relationship among education, culture, society, and politics. Likewise, religious educators who are concerned with the domesticating nature of traditional church education have taken up the quest of developing an education for political and social transformation in light of Freire's works. Even educators whose main focus is on schooling have found in his writings questions that might be raised in the contexts of institutionalized learning.

Freire has been most influential in inspiring a continuing criticism of education in many parts of the world. In the English speaking world a whole group of educators look to his ideas as a dramatic way to question what has been done in education. Critical theorists such as Henri Giroux and Ira Shor find much in his approach that approximates the types of criticisms they offer of education in advanced industrial societies. His work has inspired many to raise serious questions about schooling in both capitalist and socialist countries.

In this chapter Freire's criticism of traditional education will be presented. It is important to focus on what he finds wrong about traditional education before examining his positive proposals for educational theory and practice. Implied in his criticisms, of course, are his own values.

There are various sources for Freire's educational criticism, including his own particular social and educational philosophy and his experience as an adult educator in Brazil and other countries of the world. One important aspect of his criticism is his examination of the connection between religion and education.

RELIGIOUS AND EDUCATIONAL CRITICISM

Paulo Freire draws some of his basic assumptions from his particular religious vision and from his analysis of the role of religion in shaping education in society. Though his criticism of education is usually couched in purely secular terms, he has on occasion based it upon religious understandings. Freire recognizes that there are various religious visions that influence education in society. He asserts with confidence that his particular religious vision, the prophetic vision, is a correct one and that it leads to the proper view of education.

Freire's most complete treatment of the relationship between religion and education is found in "The Educational Role of the Churches in Latin America," an article which was first published in 1972.[1] A helpful companion article is "Education, Liberation and the Church," which has been reprinted in his *The Politics of Education*.[2] In the former article Freire describes three views of religion and compares them with the types of education to which each view is connected.

The *traditionalist* view of religion, upon which the traditional view of education is based, stresses life in the world to come. It is a religious view that urges people to reach transcendence without passing through worldliness. This type of religion fosters the closed society and is instrumental in maintaining the status quo even if this is a state of oppression. Freire classifies colonialist and missionary churches as traditionalist religious institutions. Human action in this religious view is not valued in itself but is important only as a means of gaining heaven. Proponents of traditionalist religion take a negative attitude toward the world, seeing it as a place of sin, vice, and impurity. The effect of this religious stance is not to deal with the problems of the oppressed but to point them toward a transcendent goal. Churches which preach this type of religion are havens for the masses. These churches are aligned with the ruling classes. It is easy to understand how Freire was influenced in this criticism by the writings of Marx on the conservative power of religion in society.

According to Freire, traditional religion is associated with a particular type of education. This traditional religious vision has concepts of the world, religion, human beings, and human destiny that promote an education that "will inevitably be paralyzing, alienated, and alienating."[3] This education keeps individuals from seeing their own potential for bringing about change; it is an education which is far removed from the real concerns of society; it is an education that places a great distance between individuals and their real possibilities for personal and social growth. According to Freire, the banking mode of education, which will be treated at greater length in this chapter, is a preferred educational philosophy in this type of situation. In Freire's view only a method of conscientization or critical reflection on action can free people from the dominating power of this type of education.

The second view of religion, of which Freire is also critical, is the *modernizing perspective*. Freire believes that religion in many countries of Latin America has moved in this direction. Modernization refers primarily to economic development. Industrialization has been a factor in moving societies from traditional to modern culture. While traditional religion is found most often in agricultural areas, modernizing religion develops in urban areas where modernization, industrialization, and economic development are greatest. These processes have an influence on the churches as they attempt to become more efficient and thus more bureaucratic. Modernizing churches change some of their practices, restate some of their doctrinal positions, and become more involved in problems in the social, political, and economic orders. But these churches, according to Freire, only take halfway measures which are not adequate to bring about the truly radical changes that are necessary to restructure society. These churches still remain committed to the power elite. They may speak about the *poor* or *underprivileged* but not of the *oppressed,* since the latter term attempts to explain the situation in terms that place blame on both institutions and individuals for the plight of those who suffer.

Modernizing religion also has its own particular perspective on education. Although it speaks of a liberating education, it advocates only a change in educational techniques and a change in individuals, rather than the drastic reforms of society that are necessary. This kind of education means no more than "liberating students from their blackboards, static classes, and textbook curricula, and offering them projectors and other audio-visual accessories, more dynamic classes and a new technico-professional instruction."[4] It would appear that Freire's description of liberating education is much tamer than modernizing religion, for modernizing religion takes a more political approach to problems in society by moving beyond purely church or religious concerns.

Freire's preferred kind of religion is a *prophetic* religion which commits itself to the liberation of the dominated classes and seeks the transformation of society in a radical manner. He contends that churches which embrace this form of religion have appeared in Latin America. These utopian and hopeful movements have severed ties with the power elites. They are committed to an earthly liberation, which is their concept of transcendence and salvation. These churches dare to be prophetic in presenting a critical analysis of societal structures. They define salvation in more worldly terms. For many adherents to prophetic religion, this view of religion entails recognizing at times the necessity of violent revolution. This type of religion invites members to a new Exodus or passage from oppression to liberation. The theology of such churches is the theology of liberation that speaks to the situation of the dependent, exploited, and oppressed.

Like the other forms of religion, prophetic religion is associated with a form of education which can be called both prophetic and liberating. The education that accords with this vision of religion, church, and theology "must be an instrument of transforming action, a political praxis at the service of permanent human liberation."[5] Freire makes this statement about the prophetic view of education:

> From the prophetic point of view, it makes little difference in what specific area education happens; it will always be an effort to clarify

the concrete context in which the teacher-students and student-teachers are educated and are united by their presence in action. It will always be a demythologizing praxis.[6]

What distinguishes prophetic education from traditionalist education is that prophetic education dares to make judgments about the oppressive social structures in society and involves itself in a political program for bringing about objective and radical changes in these structures. This form of education is thus concerned with criticizing the myths which keep people oppressed and with involving persons in concrete action to deal with forms of oppression.

In Freire's work as consultant to the World Council of Churches, he more fully developed the bonds that exist between his theological and his educational theories. The more he read theologians of liberation, the more he began to see that there were definite connections between this theology and his pedagogy of liberation. Just as liberation theology includes a criticism of traditional theology, so Freire's pedagogy of liberation includes a criticism of traditional education.

Freire's approach to educational criticism thus includes attention to an element that one does not usually find among educational writers: the power of religious cultures and institutions to shape education in a particular country. Freire's educational views were developed in countries in which religious values played a major role in education. This accounts in part for his special sensitivity in this matter.

To be sure, Freire clearly connects his educational criticisms and proposals to his religious vision. In appealing to the prophetic tradition he drew on biblical sources upon which many thinkers have based powerful claims for basic human rights. Such an appeal has been made by many reformers in various periods of history. There is, however, a serious problem in setting oneself up as a prophet. It is the tremendous burden of convincing others that one speaks "the Word of the Lord." It is always difficult to distinguish the true from the false prophets. One must beware of the person who wears the mantle of the prophet and whose evocative ideas do not necessarily lead to human betterment.

Therefore, in dealing with Freire it is important to recognize that very often he takes on the pose and language of the prophet. The prophet makes statements and issues judgments but does not often argue and give reasons. Freire, like a prophet, often speaks and writes in an authoritative way without offering arguments for his position. He often tends to see issues in black and white terms; his writings often deal in setting up dichotomies. Often his style of writing becomes sermonic and exhortatory. At times he exudes an air of certainty in his condemnations that reminds one of his biblical forerunners.

Notwithstanding the problems with Freire's prophetic utterances, it is important to look at his criticisms of educational practice and theorizing. In order to organize Freire's educational critique I will group his denunciations around three main themes: liberty or freedom, equality, and fraternity or fellowship. These concepts, used as the rallying cries of many political reformers and revolutionaries, have deep religious roots, even though these same principles have often been violated by religious groups and institutions. The Christian gospel, to which Freire has remained committed, emphasizes the importance of the *freedom* of the sons and daughters of the Lord in the face of every effort, both religious and secular, to enslave them. *Equality* before God, who is no respecter of persons, is a value that is found both implicitly and explicitly in religious sources, though at times it is also true that religions have justified castes and classes. Finally, *fraternity,* communion, or fellowship is most often the self-proclaimed and distinguishing characteristic of religious groups, describing both their inner life and attesting to others the worth of this particular religious commitment and community.

CALL TO FREEDOM

Freire's criticism of education is made in the name of freedom, meaning freedom for the oppressed, and freedom from repressive and manipulative forms of education.

There is no idea that Freire uses more often than freedom and words associated with it: liberation, emancipation, and empowerment. His pedagogy of the oppressed is also referred to as a pedagogy for liberation. This is the kind of language one expects from a radical or revolutionary educator.

Freire was aware that many individuals have a fear of freedom, something which he learned early as an adult literacy educator. He learned that it takes courage to take the risks of freedom and not to take the easy escape to the security of being under the control of others. For Freire true humanization comes about only if individuals are free to become what they want or should become. Recognizing that freedom is not a gift but rather something to be acquired by conquest, Freire asserts:

> [Freedom] must be pursued constantly and responsibly. Freedom is not an ideal located outside of man; nor is it an idea which becomes myth. It is rather the indispensable condition for the quest of humanization.[7]

To exercise freedom individuals must, according to Freire, perceive the limit situations and contradictions in their lives and be empowered to struggle both to transcend them and become free from them. Thus, the freedom that Freire is most concerned with is the freedom from any form of oppression, especially economic, political, and cultural.

With this type of freedom in mind, Freire subjects traditional education to a scathing criticism on the ground that it assaults basic human freedom. He calls this education "banking education" because it reduces education to "an act of depositing, in which the students are the depositories and the teacher is the depositor."[8] The only role of the students in this education is to receive, file, and store the deposits made by teachers. What is wrong about this form of education is that it "transforms students into receiving objects. It attempts to control thinking and action, leads men to adjust to the world, and inhibits their creative power."[9] Banking education for Freire is an act of domination since it indoctrinates students to adapt themselves to the world of oppression and not to challenge forces which manipulate them.

Freire proposes a liberating or problem-posing education in opposition to banking education. In liberating education, students are on equal terms with their teachers in developing the problems that are to be investigated. A fuller explanation of this educational theory and practice will be presented in the next chapter.

The importance of freedom in Freire's criticism of education is indicated by the fact that he describes the entire educational process as cultural action for freedom. This action is one in which a group of people, through dialogue, come to realize the concrete situation in which they live, the reasons for this situation, and the possible solutions to their problems. In order for action to be authentic, the participants must be free to create the curriculum along with the teacher.

Freire's analysis of banking education as destructive of human freedom is close to being the classic criticism of all didactic and teacher-centered forms of education. There is a great deal of truth in many of the criticisms he has made. Teacher-centered and book-centered education do present a particular world view to students. In situations of great oppression, as Freire describes in Brazil and elsewhere, this form of education leads persons to accept without criticism the values and positions of the dominant culture.

Yet Freire's dichotomous analysis of education into either education for freedom or for domestication does blur many important distinctions. This analysis exaggerates both the weaknesses of education for cultural transmission and the strengths of education by problem posing. All education to some degree entails a transmission of a culture, a tradition, and a history. There is a way to do this that is oppressive and there is a way to do it that is liberating. Freire is also not sufficiently critical of the perhaps more manipulative elements of his own pedagogy, as will be explained later.

A more balanced view of education sees the process as involved in a tension or dialectic between cultural transmission and cultural criticism. The debate over these two primary modes of education has raged for at least a century in the United States. In many ways Freire takes a view similar to John Dewey, who placed more importance on new knowledge rather than on the value of history and literature of the past for dealing with present problems. What Freire adds to this discussion is the analysis of what knowledge of the past, that is history and literature, does to human consciousness and consequently human freedom

EQUALITY

Freire criticizes education in the name of equality, which he connects with the virtue or concept of justice. The struggle of the oppressed is for both freedom and justice. In Freire's analysis what provokes the oppressors to violence and what leads to the dehumanization of the oppressed is the oppressors' determination to preserve an unjust social order.[10] Class-promoted injustice leads to death, despair, and poverty.

Freire clearly places the blame for unjust social orders on capitalism. He recounts his shock when he first realized how Brazilian society was divided into different classes with "millionaires living a very good life while millions of people were hungry, eating nothing."[11] Since Freire would not accept the belief that God was the author of this inequality, as had been proposed, he began a study of the historical causes for such a situation, which led him to a study of Marx and economics.

In proposing an egalitarian and socialist ideal for society, Freire is severely critical of the great disparities that exist in modern societies in the areas of wealth, power, and status. Although he speaks mainly in the context of Third World countries, where these disparities are indeed great, Freire also sees basic inequalities in advanced technological countries. In these "advanced societies" people accept the myth which projects technology "as all-powerful, beyond all structures, accessible only to a few privileged men."[12]

Freire makes it clear that his criticism of education is not limited to a rejection of traditional educational methods nor to the traditional teacher-student relationship but "extends to criticism of the capitalist system itself."[13] Freire pinpoints unequal education as one of the factors that maintains inequality in society. He also accepts the Marxist analysis according to which unequal relationships in society are mirrored in the world of education, notably in the teacher-student relationship. For him it is the domesticating power of education that prevents people from seeing the true social reality of their lives, thus forcing them to accept the inequalities in which they live. Although Freire's major focus is on adult education, he has come to see the school as an important institution that prevents the existence of a classless society.

Freire is relentless in his analysis of the inequality in the teacher-student relationship. It is this relationship which mirrors the oppression found in society. It is the teacher who speaks, knows everything, thinks, acts, disciplines, makes choices about content, has authority, and is initiator or subject. The unknowing student is acted upon, taught, disciplined, and treated as a mere object. In all these ways Freire criticizes the great distance between the teacher and the student.

Freire's criticism of education on the basis of inequality makes him a comrade of many historians, philosophers, and sociologists who have made similar criticisms. His work has been compared especially to radical sociologists of education, who consider him close to their position. His ideas echo the concepts of many neo-Marxist analysts of education.[13]

The same kinds of questions can be raised about Freire's call for more equal relationships between teacher and taught and about his call for more equality in society. There is little doubt that he has rightly pointed to the existence of inequality in society and the manifestation of it in education. Yet he still may have exaggerated the role of education both in bringing this situation about and in bringing it to an end. In his more recent works he appears a bit more sophisticated about the potential of education than he was in *Pedagogy* and other writings.

While sensitive to capitalist abuses in society, Freire has rarely, if ever, directed criticism at the abuses in socialist regimes. From reading him one would expect that the ushering in of the New Man and New Woman in the new socialist society would put an end to inequalities both in economic distribution and educational relationships. There is little evidence that this is so. Socialist regimes and their educational systems suffer from many of the same inequalities. If Freire's ideas in this area are viewed as prophetic statements, calls to arms, or manifestoes, they have some validity. Scrutinized as serious educational and social theory, they lack both the common sense and empirical evidence necessary to be substantiated.

Freire's presentation of the traditional teacher-student relationship also appears exaggerated and one sided. Pushed to its logical conclusion his theory eliminates the role of the teacher by almost assuming there is nothing to teach. While some of his criticisms ring true as prophetic statements, they cannot bear careful scrutiny. While in some areas of education students are in possession of knowledge which a coordinator needs only to bring out, there are large areas which entail careful teaching and even testing.

FRATERNITY

Finally, Freire's criticism of education is made in the name of fraternity. The term embraces the quality of the relationship that should exist among persons in society. Fraternity refers to a certain equality of social esteem, the absence of manners of deference and servility, and a sense of civic friendship and social solidarity.[15] The ideal of fraternity involves bonds of sentiment and feeling. True fraternity exists in society when its institutions enrich the personal and social lives of its citizens. The demands of fraternity are not easily separated from the demands for freedom and equality.

The term that Freire uses for the ideal of fraternity is communion, a word that has deep religious meaning within the Christian faith, referring to the Christian's spiritual and symbolic union with the founder and also to the spiritual union that exists among members of the Christian faith. For Freire, fraternal solidarity is essential for religious, political, and educational salvation or liberation. He makes the parallel himself:

> Men free themselves only in concert, in communion, collaborating on something that they want to correct. There is an interesting theological parallel to this: no one saves another, no one saves himself all alone; because only in communion can we save ourselves or not save ourselves.[16]

For Freire educational fraternity or communion in Brazil was threatened by a "rigidly authoritarian structure of life which formed and strengthened an anti-democratic mentality."[17] The Brazilian tradition, he asserts, was not one of working *with* the students, but one of working *on* them.[18] For the failure of efforts for democratic reform in Brazil, Freire blames the type of relationship that exists in Brazilian society, particularly the master-slave relationships analyzed by Gilberto Freyre. Since he found the same type of relationship between teacher and students, he argued that such an authoritative social organization prevented the development of a sense of fraternity essential for life in a democratic society.

Freire's attack on "banking education" is shaped by the ideal of communion that he espouses. This form of education denies fraternity because in it, according to Freire, the teacher is the subject of the learning process, while the students are mere objects. The pupil is in a position of subservience and must pay deference to the teacher. The student is not admitted to true partnership in learning in this form of education. No solidarity exists between teacher and pupils because there is no true communication upon which solidarity is based. Banking education "stimulates the credulity of students, with the ideological intent (often not perceived by educators) of indoctrinating them to adapt to the world of oppression."[19] Freire contends that his liberating pedagogy based on respect, communication, and solidarity is essential for a democratic education in a democratic society.

What prevents true fraternity or communion in society, for Freire, is the absence of dialogue, which he makes essential to his educational and social theory. If people are not free, if they do not meet others as equals, they cannot be in communion or dialogue with one another. What offends true fraternity in society are actions which are "antidialogical." Freire gives some examples. Actions of conquest, such as were prevalent in Latin American history, reduced persons to things to be conquered. Actions of those in power to divide and rule others also offend the norms for fraternity. Manipulations of the masses are efforts to force the people to conform to the will of leaders. The worst violation is cultural invasion where attempts are made to violently disabuse individuals of their culture by imposing another, supposedly superior, culture on them.

It is hard to disagree with Freire's criticism on grounds of fraternity or communion. What he points out are many of the ills that have plagued all societies, no matter what the political or economic arrangements. One can find many of these same abuses in theocracies, where people are supposedly under the rule of God. One can raise questions, however, about how Freire deals with these issues. His proposals of communion with the people and dialogic action seem inadequate to address these problems. Here, as elsewhere, Freire adopts the singlemindedness of the prophet or revolutionary in pointing to a simple solution. By doing so he apparently underestimates the difficulty of the task and overestimates the means he has presented. Perhaps this was the kind of rhetoric he assumed was called for in what he considered prerevolutionary Brazil. Perhaps it is the Latin American mode of expression and discourse. While the words are indeed inspiring, one is left with little more than inspiration to face the great tasks of bringing about a more civil society in the face of intransigent evils.

Freire's criticism of education has had great influence around the world. In every country liberal and radical educators draw on his writings in offering criticisms of society and in proposing educational and social reforms. From the very beginning, however, critics have argued that there is nothing original in his ideas. In an early work Freire responded to his critics:

In the campaigns carried out against me . . . it was said that I was not the "inventor of dialogue" (as if I had ever made such an irresponsible affirmation). It was said that I had done "nothing original," and that I had "plagiarized European or North American educators," as well as the author of a Brazilian primer. On the subject of originality. I have always agreed with Dewey, for whom originality does not lie in the "extraordinary and fanciful," but in "putting everyday things to uses which had not occurred to others."[20]

Whether Freire's criticisms of education are original or not, one thing can be asserted with certainty: his criticisms were timely and effective. Freire's critique of educational theory and practice has struck a responsive chord throughout the world. What needs to be developed are his positive proposals for a pedagogy of liberation.

NOTES

1. Paulo Freire. "The Educational Role of the Churches in Latin America." Washington, D.C.: LADOC, 3, 14. 1972.
2. Paulo Freire. "Education, Liberation, and the Church." *Risk,* Vol., IX, No. 1, 1973, pp. 34–38; reprinted in *The Politics of Education.* South Hadley, Mass.: Bergin and Garvey, 1985.
3. Paulo Freire. *The Politics of Education,* p. 133.
4. Paulo Freire. *The Politics of Education,* p. 137.
5. Paulo Freire. *The Politics of Education,* p. 140.
6. Paulo Freire. *The Politics of Education,* p. 140.
7. Paulo Freire. *Pedagogy of the Oppressed.* New York: Continuum, 1970, p. 31.
8. Paulo Freire. *Pedagogy,* p. 58.
9. Paulo Freire. *Pedagogy,* p. 71.
10. Paulo Freire. *Pedagogy,* p. 28.
11. Ira Shor and Paulo Freire. *A Pedagogy for Liberation.* South Hadley, Mass.: Bergin and Garvey, 1987, p. 47.
12. Paulo Freire. *Pedagogy,* p. 37.
13. Paulo Freire and Antonio Faundez. *Learning to Question: A Pedagogy of Liberation.* New York: Continuum, 1989, p. 45.
14. Henry Giroux. "Introduction to Paulo Freire." *The Politics of Education.*
15. John Rawls. *A Theory of Justice.* Cambridge, Mass.: Harvard University Press, 1971, p. 105.

16. Paulo Freire. "Conscientizing as a Way of Liberating." Washington, D.C.: LADOC, 2, 29c, 1972, p. 8.
17. Paulo Freire. *Education for Critical Consciousness*. New York: Continuum, 1973, p. 26.
18. Paulo Freire. *Education for Critical Consciousness*, p. 38.
19. Paulo Freire. *Pedagogy*, 1970, p. 65.
20. Paulo Freire. *Education for Critical Consciousness*, p. 5.

CHAPTER 9

An Educational Theory for Liberation

Freire has thus far been basically presented in this book as a Christian humanist, a Christian-Marxist social critic, a Marxist revolutionary theorist, and a radical critic of education. One last area remains to be treated: his constructive educational theory. This theory, which has had great influence in both First and Third World countries, has been subject to rather thorough criticism in the past twenty years.

The task of explaining Freire's educational theory is not an easy one. Like most utopian thinkers, he is much clearer in his criticism and in what he rejects than in the constructive educational theory which he proposes. Vagueness sets in when he makes positive proposals and attempts to describe what education or learning should be in utopian societies. There are, however, sufficient indications in his writings to develop the essential elements of an educational theory.

Freire's educational theory fits into the mold of normative or prescriptive theory. Such a theory of education includes statements about aims, principles, and methods as they are and as they should be; some data based on empirical fact; and metaphysical, epistemological or theological assumptions.[1] This type of theory differs from the analytic approach to educational philosophy which has become prevalent in the English speaking world, found most representatively in the work of R. S. Peters and Israel Scheffler. One finds in Freire's writings some analysis of concepts, but this is clearly secondary to the normative statements he makes about education, learning, knowing, aims, content, and methods. He is clearly concerned with prescribing what education should and should not be.

121

In the course of this chapter I will make some criticisms of Freire's educational theory. This is not to deny the power of the method of literacy and postliteracy education that Freire and others have practiced. My concern will be more in analyzing and criticizing the theory which he presents to explain this educational practice.

FREIRE'S THEORY OF LEARNING

The central concept in Freire's educational theory is the concept of conscientization. In the past twenty-five years, Freire has been more closely associated with this term than any other Latin American educator. Freire tells us that the word was born during a series of round table meetings of professors at the Brazilian Institute of Higher Studies in 1964. Freire does not know exactly who coined the term, but he tells us that when he heard it, be became fully convinced that "education, as an exercise in freedom, is an act of knowing, a critical approach to reality. It was inevitable that the word became a part of the terminology I used thereafter to express my pedagogical views and it easily came to be thought of as something I had created."[2]

Freire has now expressed some reservations about using the term because of the many misunderstandings that abound and the many usages to which it has been put. He is so identified with the term, however, that he cannot be disassociated from it, just as John Dewey cannot be separated from progressive education even though he became its severest critic.

There is clearly a development in Freire's concept of conscientization. In his first book, *Education for Critical Consciousness,* critical consciousness is described as critical reflection by which a person can know the true causes of things as they are, a process to be accomplished through dialogue and codifications of reality. In *Pedagogy* and other later works the concept becomes more radical and more political. It now entails the denunciation of certain realities and the announcement of new realities through praxis. Freire associates the word with the Marxist concept of praxis, a term not found in the earlier work.

In his early work Freire described conscientization as the development of critical awareness through dialogical educational programs concerned with social and political responsibilities.[3] The purpose of this process is to bring about critical attitudes in people. These critical attitudes are to lead to the transformation of the world. He calls this democratic education, for it is founded on faith in humans, on the belief that persons not only can discuss the problems of their country but also that they have the power to solve these problems. Conscientization includes exchanges of ideas, debates, discussions, and working *with* students and not *on* them.[4]

Freire fashions conscientization as a process that results from confrontation with the world; it also entails constant research as well as invention and reinvention. It is built upon the relations between human beings and the world which are relations of transformation. Conscientization perfects itself through placing a critical focus on these problems. Conscientization for Freire is not an individual but a social task. It is also never neutral, for the educator has the right to have opinions, but he must not impose them on others.[5]

In *Pedagogy* Freire gives a fuller explanation of conscientization, describing it as a form of co-intentional education, in which students and teachers co-intend reality, that is, both are subjects in critically unveiling reality and in recreating knowledge.[6] This process receives a more philosophical explanation in *Pedagogy*. Conscientization takes place in

> a learning situation in which the cognizable object (far from being the end of the cognitive act) intermediates the cognitive actors— teachers and students. The student-teacher contradiction must be resolved in order to have dialogic relations, in order to have true education. The teacher is also taught through dialogue with his students. No one teaches another, nor is anyone self-taught. Men teach each other, mediated by the world, by the cognizable objects.[7]

Perhaps the best definition of what Freire means by conscientization is contained in an editor's footnote in *Cultural Action for Freedom*. Conscientization there is defined as "the process in which men, not as recipients, but as knowing subjects achieve a deepening awareness both of the sociocultural reality which shapes their lives, and of their capacity to transform that reality through action upon it."[8] Conscientization thus includes two moments: an awareness of the social and cultural situation in which one lives and an awareness of one's ability to change situations through actions.

Freire has in many of his writings shown himself sensitive to the charge that his position is an idealistic one, comparable to the

French *prise de conscience,* which is tantamount to intellectual en-lightenment. Those who read his early work can see the justification for this charge against him. Freire contends, however, that conscien-tization goes deeper than this because it penetrates to what reality really is and because it is connected with praxis. Freire's concept of praxis—social action plus reflection—depends upon the Marxist concept of praxis. Conscientization demands a historical commit-ment; it demands involvement and intervention with reality. For Freire, then, conscientization does not create reality, but merely discovers it. In Marxist terms, which he is fond of using, conscienti-zation entails both the denouncing of an oppressive reality and the announcing of a liberating reality. Freire thus uses the phenomeno-logical thrust in order to avoid idealism and materialism by attempt-ing to forge a third way to explain knowing, which is both objective and subjective.

RELIGIOUS INTERPRETATION OF CONSCIENTIZATION

Freire uses religious language and symbolism to explain his central notion of conscientization. Conscientization is compared to the Easter experience of Jesus' death and resurrection. For Freire, "the teacher has to live the profound meaning of Easter."[9] To do this teachers must die as the exclusive educators of students and learners must die to the role of exclusive learners of educators. This dying is necessary so that both can be reborn as real learners. It is this death and rebirth that makes education for freedom possible. In existentialist terms the educator must be *present* to students but not be *the presence* itself.

For educators to experience the meaning of Easter, they "must die as elitists so as to be resurrected on the side of the oppressed, that they be born again with the beings who were not allowed to be."[10] Freire enumerates the myths that teachers must die to, including

> the myth of their superiority, of their purity of soul, of their virtues, their wisdom, the myth that they save the poor, the myth of the neutrality of the church, of theology, education, science, technology, the myth of their own impartiality. . . . of the inferiority of the peo-ple, of their [the poor's] spiritual and physical impurity, and of the absolute ignorance of the oppressed.[11]

Freire identifies these myths as manifestations of the bourgeois mentality.

Just as the real Easter was not something merely symbolic but involved praxis and was a part of history, so the educator's Easter will lead to a changed consciousness only if it is existentially experienced. Thus Freire attempts to guard against a merely spiritualist interpretation of his words.

The Easter experience is used to explain not only the new relationship that should exist between teachers and learners but the very act of learning itself. Death and rebirth are implicit in Freire's primary metaphor of denouncing one reality and announcing a new reality through the activity of praxis. This imagery, which he takes from the Polish Marxist humanist Kolakowski, echoes the experience of Easter and the conversion that the followers of Jesus should go through. Conversion entails a radical change in a person's consciousness, something to be achieved primarily through some concrete action or involvement.

This use of religious symbolism to explain conscientization illustrates the point made earlier about Freire becoming more religious as he becomes more radical. This religious symbolism is not found in his earlier work when he was under the influence of Christian democracy. The religious symbolism is connected to the Marxist interpretation of conscientization.

LEVELS OF CONSCIENTIZATION

Critical to understanding Freire's conception of conscientization is his theory of the various levels of consciousness. The terminology he uses for explaining these levels comes from grammar, a subject which has always fascinated Freire since his days as a teacher of Portuguese. Because Freire elaborates these levels in relationship to the development of Brazilian society, these levels have a strong social and historical character. The levels can also be applied to the development of individual consciousness so long as one insists on the social character of knowledge. Freire gives two explanation of these levels, one in *Education for Critical Consciousness* and one in *Pedagogy*. In the latter explanation he uses Marxist terminology.

The lowest level of consciousness Freire calls *semi-intransitive consciousness*. (It is called intransitive because the persons who possess it are scarcely subjects who know objects or things in the world.) This level prevails in closed societies of the past and even in backwards regions today. People with this consciousness are preoccupied with meeting their most elementary needs and are immersed in reality. Characterized by the near absence of historical consciousness, they are practically impervious to problems and challenges beyond the biological sphere. They are immersed in a one-dimensional oppressive present. The relationships that they are involved in have shaped their sociocultural situation and cannot be comprehended by them. Fatalism is a prevalent characteristic of this consciousness. It is marked by an involvement in magic and religious rites.

In his earlier work Freire attributed this form of consciousness to the general cultural condition in which individuals lived. In later writings he gives a definite Marxist interpretation. According to Freire, semi-intransitive consciousness is the consciousness of people who are dominated, dependent, and oppressed, and who live in closed societies which are dominated by other countries. In the context of Latin America the control has come from Spain, Portugal, and now the United States. Freire terms these cultures the "cultures of silence." This type of consciousness is prevalent in the emerging societies of the Third World. Persons at this level take the facts of their sociocultural situation as "givens." This form of consciousness is also characterized by a fatalistic mentality, which views all of life as related to destiny or fortune, that is, forces beyond human control. Self-depreciation is a most common attribute of this level of consciousness, for people at this level have internalized the negative values that the dominant culture ascribes to them. This level of consciousness is also marked by excessive emotional dependence to such a degree that to be is to be under someone, to depend on another. This form of consciousness often expresses itself in defensive and therapeutic magic.

Naive or *semitransitive consciousness* is the second level of consciousness. (The consciousness is transitive since individuals are beginning to become subjects who can dialogue with others.) In earlier writings this is described as a consciousness that sees problems but oversimplifies them. It does not seek to investigate thoroughly. It has an emotional style, the consciousness of a mass of people who are only beginning to dialogue.

In his Marxist reinterpretation Freire explains that silence is not the characteristic of this level since a serious questioning of one's life situation begins, albeit at a naive and primitive level. This consciousness is more likely to judge the cultural situation as determined by human activity. People in this state of development, however, are easily swayed by populist leaders. Although they may begin to have some control over their lives, the danger of manipulative leadership is ever present. Freire also terms this level *popular consciousness* because of its connection with populist leadership.

There is some form of elitism implied in Freire's analysis of consciousness, which emerges in his description of the lowest levels. This blind spot is one of the main charges that Peter Berger levels against the theory.[12] Freire never makes clear how this analysis is related with his more revolutionary writings, where he asserts the great wisdom and intelligence of the masses.

Before we pass to Freire's description of the highest level of consciousness, it may be helpful to point out the explicit Marxist character of Freire's more mature description of these levels. Like Marx, Freire explains cultural-historical reality as a superstructure in relationship to an infrastructure. The levels of consciousness of Freire correspond to the false or reifying consciousness of Marx. "Reification," for Marx, is the viewing of the products of human activity as if they were products of nature, cosmic laws, or divine will. The reified world is thus a dehumanized world since the real relationship between humans and the world is reversed in the knowing process. Humans are viewed as the product of a world which they, in fact, have made. They are capable, paradoxically, of producing a reality that denies them. In Marxist epistemology, reification is closely allied to alienation.[13]

The highest level of consciousness for Freire is *critical consciousness,* or *critically transitive consciousness,* which is achieved through the process of conscientization. Though he does not cite Dewey, this consciousness is similar to Dewey's critical reflection. This level is marked by depth in the interpretation of problems, self-confidence in discussions, receptiveness to other ideas, and refusal to shirk responsibility. The quality of discourse here is clearly dialogical. At this level, persons scrutinize their own thoughts and see proper causal and circumstantial correlations between events. This is the consciousness found in authentically democratic regimes. While the movement from level one to level two can occur through such processes as urbanization and industrialization, the achievement of critical transitivity requires "an active, dialogical educational program concerned with social and political responsibility, and prepared to avoid the danger of massification."[14]

In his Marxist reinterpretation Freire describes conscientization in the context of Third World countries as entailing a radical denunciation of dehumanizing structures and the announcement of a new reality to be created by liberated persons. Conscientization demands a rigorous and rational critique of the ideology that supports oppressive structures. Critical consciousness is brought about not through intellectual efforts alone but through praxis, the authentic union of action and reflection. The fact that people are moving towards this form of consciousness provokes threatened power elites to react violently as they did in Brazil in 1964.

At this point a serious weakness in Freire's concept of conscientization must be indicated. Freire comes close to saying that people's knowledge of their true interests guarantees their participation in activity to achieve results. We know, however, that knowledge alone is not adequate to this task. As Horowitz rightly remarks:

> The line between action and interests is far from straight. Even if we ignore the dilemmas arising out of a direct correlation of actions and interests, there is a policy issue involved; namely, the degree of social unrest necessary to stimulate a person to think along developmental lines without creating complete revolutionary upheaval.[15]

There is a real possibility that people involved in conscientization might become even more entrenched in their thinking once they see the full impact of oppression in their lives.

THEORY OF LEARNING

After a discussion of the role of conscientization in Freire's thought, it is possible to see more clearly his theory of human learning. Learning for Freire is the process by which one moves from one level of consciousness to another. The content of each level is the view that persons have of their existence in the social world and the power that they have to determine their destiny. Learning thus begins with assessing the present level of consciousness as it manifests itself in language, self-concept, world view, and present living conditions. Becoming aware of the contingency of social reality is the beginning of learning. In other words, learning is the movement toward critical consciousness. Its basis is an awareness that there is an essential difference between the given character of the natural world and the contingency of the social world. This contingent world lies within human power to change. Learning is thus the process of challenging and being challenged by the given character of one's life situation and of the sociocultural reality in which one lives.

For Freire, learning is predominantly an active process. The process of learning begins with the learners' words, ideas, and life situation which the educator uses to codify the world in which the learners live. The task of the educator is to aid learners to examine, challenge, and criticize these situations as presented to them verbally and pictorially.

In emphasizing the activity of the learner as paramount, Freire does not blaze a new trail, for his principle has been voiced by philosophers and psychologists of education. But his strong emphasis on learning as dialogical action between learners and educators highlights a critical aspect of social learning. The adult learning process implies for him the existence of two interrelated contexts.

> One is the context of authentic dialogue between learners and educators as equally knowing subjects. This is what school should be— theoretical contexts of dialogue. The second is the real, concrete context of facts, the social reality in which men exist.[16]

Freire stresses the close connection between the two contexts. The Marxist concept of praxis as the continuing dialectical relationship between action and reflection bridges the gap between the twin contexts. A group of learners reflects on its actions in order to gain a deeper understanding of them and of their causes so that the group will be able to act differently according to its new understanding. For Freire then, learning is the total process of becoming aware of the concrete situation in which one lives, understanding how that situation came to be and how it might be changed, and then acting to change it. This conception of learning is similar to Dewey's view of learning as the reconstruction of experience. In Marxist terms, learning as conscientization is the continuing process of knowing and denouncing one reality and announcing a new reality toward which persons can strive.

Freire is interested both in the learning of individuals and groups. He makes the freedom of learners to pursue ideas essential to his educational theory. In practice, however, the individual may come under strong pressure from the group and particularly the coordinator of the group. In fact, the charge of subtle manipulation has been made of the Freire method, even though the method is designed to free individuals from dehumanizing and oppressive learning.

Freire also makes clear the political aspect of learning. In his judgment oppressive elites in the Third World use education to dominate the masses. For him learning is political because it is power for those who generate it as much as it is power for those who use it. Learning is political since in his view to learn or to know something is inseparable from deciding to change it, to preserve it, to destroy it, or to fully experience it as one's own problem.

ORGANIZATION OF LEARNING

Freire's organization of learning is similar to the method of participant observation used by anthropologists and sociologists. The various steps in this procedure can be briefly described. A team of experts studies a context to arrive at the significant themes and issues in the life of the people of an area. These themes are then codified through pictorial representations. People from the area are involved in the choice of these themes, words, and codifications. The circles of learners may have as their purpose literacy education or postliteracy or political education.

Freire terms this type of educational arrangement "problem-posing" education. He admits its similarities to the type of education proposed by Dewey and the progressives in the United States. In fact, he readily admits his dependence on democratic and liberal educators. While Freire's procedures are comparable to these educators, the same cannot be said for the theories through which he explains these procedures. Freire uses the terms and concept of existential phenomenology to explain what takes place in human consciousness and group interaction.

One deficiency with Freire's organization of learning is his exclusive dependence on the one method of dialogue. He seems to imply that any other form of education is necessarily manipulative and indoctrinating. In railing against the authoritarian education that he observed in Brazilian society, he perhaps goes to the extreme of seeing no value in lecture and direct presentation as educational methods. Moreover, he is not explicitly aware of the possibilities of subtle manipulation that exists even in "free" dialogue among students and teachers.

CRITIQUE OF FREIRE'S THEORY OF LEARNING

Freire's concept of learning as conscientization can be criticized on a number of points. One criticism has already been made, according to which Freire has been accused of excessive idealism in his description of the process of knowing. In later writings he has tried to posit a middle position between a subjectivism and a "mechanism" or between rationalism and empiricism in explaining human knowing.

Another criticism against the theory is its appeal to some sort of transcendent view of reality. Through conscientization, for Freire, individuals come to see reality as it really is. In Freire's description of his method, the group arrives at a true and authentic knowledge of the situation. One sees little awareness in his writings of the complexities of the reality with which people are attempting to grapple. In his public addresses and conversations, he appears less certain. Perhaps Freire betrays in this matter another subtle influence of his religious vision, with its absolutes about humans and nature. His view of the fixity of persons, nature, and the world conflicts with his statements about the human fashioning of history and making of culture. We may have here an example of the classical difficulty experienced by many Christian thinkers in assimilating some of the dynamic concepts of Marxist thought into the often static notions of religious thought about humans and reality.

Still, Freire's concept of learning as conscientization is valuable for a number of reasons. It is refreshing to look at a theory of human learning that has been elaborated at least partly in educational practice, that is, the literacy training method. Few have denied the success of the practice. People learned to read and write in a short period of time. The method has now been in use all over the world for twenty-five years. There is also evidence that people became critically aware of the social reality in which they had been immersed and took steps to change and control this reality. Yet success in practice does not necessarily mean truth and consistency in theory. One can inadequately explain what one has successfully practiced. Persons can also succeed because they do not practice what they theorize. Freire again and again goes back to the reality of what he did in order to explain his theory as completely as as consistently as possible. He also modified his practice as a result of theoretical and practical situations. There is in his work, therefore, the close dialectical relationship between theory and practice that lies at the very heart of his educational philosophy.

Learning for Freire is subordinated to political and social purposes. Ironically, such a theory is open to the charge of indoctrination and manipulation. The situation in which Freire worked in Brazil made him sensitive to these charges, at least to the degree of avoiding conflict with right wing elements in Brazilian society. He is even more sensitive to these charges now that his writings have been examined and considered for application to other countries and cultures. Is the Freire theory of learning necessarily indoctrinating and manipulative? A close look at his writings reveals a certain ambivalence.

Freire argues strongly against a banking concept of education wherein teachers make deposits of information into the passive minds of students. He has constantly opposed the use of primers in literacy education since he feels that these impose not only words but also a world view on students. Freire insists that the words and the themes to be used in education be those common among the people who are to be educated. The content of education is to be determined jointly with the people who are to pursue the learning. Freire also specifies that the codifications of the realities to which the words and themes refer should be neither too explicit nor too enigmatic. If the codifications are too explicit, they will take on the character of propaganda and thus prevent the development of critical awareness in learners. It they are too subtle or enigmatic, they will lose their capacity to provoke thoughtful discussion. Freire also answers the charges of indoctrination by contending that his goal is to get people to learn by having them challenge the concrete reality of their lives as presented in the codifications. Another view of social reality is not imposed on them, but through discussing a problematic situation they are led to see the true condition under which they live and also begin to see that the present social reality is not determined but can be changed.

Freire insists that his method is nonmanipulative. He contends that there is some middle ground between totally free discovery by individuals and the direct impartation of knowledge to individuals, which he views as domesticating and manipulative. He believes that dialogue is the middle ground.

Although Freire is sensitive to the charge of subtle manipulation, it cannot clearly be stated that he totally escapes this charge. For him, there is no neutral education:

> All educational practice implies a theoretical stance on the educator's part. This stance implies—sometimes more, sometimes less implicitly—an interpretation of man and the world.
> It could not be otherwise.[17]

This nonneutrality is shown in the fact that out of all the words and themes that could have been chosen for literacy and post literacy education, Freire chose those which had the greatest capacity for challenging the social reality. The process of conscientization entails for Freire a radical denunciation of dehumanizing structures, accompanied by the proclamation of a new reality to be created by humans. Freire is confident that this will come about through free dialogue in which learners and educators participate as equals. Yet is there not a subtle manipulation built into this method, given the lack of education in the students and the obvious political purposes of the teachers? In such circumstances, it would appear most difficult to satisfy the demands for objectivity and an appeal to rational argumentation.

CONCLUSION

Notwithstanding these criticisms, Freire's theory of education remains a powerful one in the development of a critical pedagogy. This pedagogy attempts to engage learners in a process of education in which all assumptions are exposed, all arguments questioned, and all conclusions evaluated by teachers and learners. Minority groups throughout the world have found in this pedagogy a powerful instrument for understanding their plight and for challenging the dominant forces in society.

NOTES

1. William K. Frankena. "A Model for Analyzing a Philosophy of Education." In Jane Martin, ed. *Readings in the Philosophy of Education*. Boston: Allyn and Bacon, 1970, p. 16.
2. Paulo Freire. "Conscientizing as a Way of Knowing." Washington, D.C.: LADOC. 1972, 2, 29, p. 1.
3. Paulo Freire. *Education for Critical Consciousness*. New York: Continuum, 1973, p. 19.
4. Paulo Freire. *Education for Critical Consciousness*, pp. 34–38.
5. Paulo Freire. *Education for Critical Consciousness*, pp., 100, 109, 148–149.
6. Paulo Freire. *Pedagogy of the Oppressed*. New York: Continuum, 1970, pp. 55–56.
7. Paulo Freire. *Pedagogy*, pp. 66–67.
8. Paulo Freire. *Cultural Action for Freedom*. Harvard Educational Review and Center for the Study of Development and Social Change, 1970, p. 27.
9. Paulo Freire. *The Politics of Education*. South Hadley, Mass.: Bergin and Garvey, 1985, p. 105.
10. Paulo Freire. *The Politics of Education*, p. 122.
11. Paulo Freire. *The Politics of Education*, p. 123.
12. Peter Berger. *Pyramids of Sacrifice*. Baltimore: Penguin, 1977.
13. Peter Berger and Thomas Luckmann. *Social Construction of Reality*. Garden City, New York: Doubleday, 1966, pp. 200–201.
14. Paulo Freire. *Education for Critical Consciousness*. New York: Seabury, 1973, p. 19.
15. Irving Louis Horowitz. *Three Worlds of Development*. New York: Oxford University Press, 1966, p. 295.
16. Paulo Freire. *Cultural Action for Freedom*, p. 14.
17. Paulo Freire. *Cultural Action for Freedom*, p. 6.

CHAPTER 10

Theologian of Liberation and Education

Paulo Freire is primarily an adult educator. Yet to explain his comprehensive view of education over the past twenty-five years he had been driven to draw on many academic disciplines, notably philosophy, social theory, and political theory. One of the richest sources for his analysis has been his religious vision and theological views. Having treated other aspects of Freire's thought in a systematic form, I will direct my attention in this final chapter to Freire's theological views. In many chapters of the book I have already made connections between Freire's religious views and other parts of his theory; therefore, there will be some repetition in this chapter. I believe that this is justified in order to present an organized account of Freire's theological views. Freire has entered into serious dialogue with Christian theologians by relating his theories to theological concepts. Moreover, many theologians have shown keen interest in his work.

Freire is certainly not a theologian in a professional sense of someone trained in theology whose primary academic reference group is theologians. Yet on a number of occasions he has entered into the theological arena in talks and writings. He himself explains his theological interest:

> Although I am no theologian, I line up with those who do not find theology an anachronism, but recognize that it has a vital function to perform. And to fulfill that task, the theologian should take, as the starting point in his reflection, the history of man.[1]

For Freire the starting point of theology is the concrete life of individuals, and its purpose is to aid in the task of combatting unjust

135

structures and working for just ones. Although Freire considers himself only an onlooker intrigued by theology, he can certainly be classified as a theologian in the public sense of the term, as one who takes interest in theology and who occasionally writes from this perspective.

A THEOLOGIAN OF LIBERATION

Freire in a number of his writings identifies himself with *liberation or political theology*.[2] Such a theology, in his description, speaks to involvement with the liberation of the oppressed. Recognizing that the oppressed can become instruments of transforming society, this theology issues a call to all Christians, especially those in Third World countries, to be revolutionaries in society. This theology also deals realistically with the issue of political involvement, even to the point of proposing violent revolutionary activity. The theology of liberation, moreover, puts special stress on some neglected elements in the Christian tradition: politics, utopia, the liberator God, and the prophetic church. It also leads to a reinterpretation of many traditional Christian symbols.

Freire recognizes the need for the theological rebirth which began with liberation theology. Only this type of theology, he says, enables us to overcome the jolt of the Death of God theology that spelled the end of a medieval theology that is still current in many parts of the church. Liberation theology has the capacity of making the church more relevant to the social and political fabric of society. In Freire's view traditional academic theology, long identified as a force for justifying existing social arrangements, does not have the power to challenge such arrangements when they are unjust.

Freire, like many liberation theologians, draws on the important contribution of Marxist social and political analysis. Many Latin American scholars, including theologians, turned to Marx to find an explanation for the ills that beset their societies and for possible economic, social, and political alternatives. Not unaware of the many distortions of Marxist thought and corruption in Marxist societies, Freire draws on the humanist writings of the early Marx. The appropriation of some Marxist concepts by Freire and liberation theologians has caused them to come under suspicion by church authorities and traditional theologians.

Freire describes his theology as a *utopian* or *prophetic theology*, a theology of hope, one which both denounces oppression and oppressors and announces a transformed world. This theology, he contends, must denounce the bourgeoisie and announce the coming of the new person in the new society. He contrasts this theology, which contains prophecy and hope, to traditional theology, which dichotomizes the world and encourages persons to passively await a better life hereafter.[3] It is Freire's view that liberation theology calls the church back to its historical vocation—to be critical and prophetic with regard to the world and not to adapt or bend to pressures by making concessions to unjust situations. He comments that his position is to be identified with

> a church that must not forget it is called by its origins to die shivering in the cold. This is a utopia, it is a denunciation and an announcement with a historical commitment that adds up to a heroism in life.[4]

Freire also calls his theology *anthropological* since its starting point must be the actual life of individuals in the world. By beginning at this point theology can better lead to cultural action for freedom and to conscientization.[5] Though liberation theology takes account of the Christian tradition and texts, it does not start with them since starting with the texts runs the risk of remaining with them and not moving to real problems in the world. As in other areas, Freire is fearful of the effect of a too strong commitment to texts, philosophies, and structures of the past. It is usually these past forms that erect barriers to authentic human freedom.

Freire has great hopes for the Third World theology of liberation since it encourages liberation theologians and all Christians to be men and women of the world. They are also encouraged to be the hopeful persons and the prophets of that society who can aid in breaking down old structures and building up new ones. They can aid all Christians to recover their vocation to challenge injustice and oppression in society.

A THEOLOGY OF HOPE

Another main theme in Freire's theological vision is hope or utopia. In his "Letter to a Theology Student" Freire develops the theme that theology should present grounds for Christians to be hopeful in this world. Freire presents an active view of hope, identifying it not with passive waiting, compromise, or accommodation. He rather describes hope as involved in the dialectic of restlessness and peace which are entailed in all human searching.

Hope for Freire is related to utopia, which is explained in terms of denouncing unjust structures and announcing free and just social arrangements. In fact, the process of conscientization can be explained in essence as an activity of hope and utopia. For Freire hope is to be identified not with mere waiting but with searching. Humans are active creatures whose natural tendency is toward action and transformation. In fact, human salvation comes from a conversion marked by a questing, a salvation that is achieved by our own efforts. Rejecting any fatalistic acceptance of the status quo, and rejecting the dichotomy between worldliness and otherworldliness, Freire sees the Christian task as working with God to complete the work of creation by removing all elements of injustice.

GOD AND PERSONS

The primary theological symbol in Christianity is God and God's relationship to persons and history. Freire, like liberation theologians, accepts the existence of God without attempting to offer any proof for it. Freire recognizes that human understanding of God is an extremely important part of theological training which he thinks should include cultural action for liberation so that persons can

> get rid of their ingenuous concept of God (it is a myth that alienates them) and get a new notion of Him in which God, as a presence in history, does not in the slightest keep persons from "making history"—the history of their liberation.[6]

Thus in Freire's view God empowers men and women to make history through their liberating efforts.

In presenting this new concept of God, Freire describes God as *Creator* and *Liberator:*

> God's relationship over us is based on the fact of our finitude and our knowledge of this finitude. For we are incomplete beings, and the completeness of our incompleteness is encountered in our very relationship with our Creator, a relationship which by its very nature,

can never be a relationship of domination or domestication, but is always a relationship of liberation. Thus religion (from *religare*—to bind) which incarnates this transcendent relationship among humans should never be an instrument of alienation. Precisely because humans are finite and indigent beings, in this transcendence through love, humans have their return to their source, who liberates them.[7]

The context of these words is Freire's description of the basic nature of persons who are to be educated. His argument is that human nature includes a capacity to transcend one's limit situations, especially if they are situations of domination, alienation, and oppression. The basic reason persons are enabled to do this is their relationship to God. Recognizing that this relationship cannot be described totally in terms of a Creator-creature relationship, Freire adds the significant element of *liberation* to describe this relationship. The liberation he refers to is one from alienation, domination, and oppression, thus not a purely spiritual liberation, but one which is rooted in the concrete historical situations of human existence. Freire is opposed to any religious view that would make "an unfeasible separation between humanity and transcendence."[8]

Although he does not develop the idea, Freire seems to attach to his notion of God as Liberator the concept of a "limited God" described by process theologians. He states that "God, the Absolute, limits Himself by seeing some value in men—limited, unfinished, and incompleted as they are—as beings that choose, as sharers in His creative work."[9] God is limited in the sense that God uses or needs the freely chosen cooperation of humans to bring about the completion of a just world.

Human relationships, for Freire, should mirror relationships between humans and God in that they are marked by freedom. The relationships between persons and their creator or source are also ones that continues throughout life. The quality in humans which enables them to transcend even the most deplorable life situation is the capacity to love.

Freire further describes the relationship between human beings and God as a *dialogical* one in which God is a continuing and lifelong partner to dialogue with human beings. Freire explains:

Transitivity of consciousness makes a person "permeable." It leads one to replace a disengagement from existence with almost total engagement. Existence is a dynamic concept, implying eternal dialogue between person and person, between a person and the world, between a person and Creator. It is this dialogue which makes a person an historical being.[10]

As noted earlier, there is no more important concept in Freire's theory of education than dialogue. The important point that Freire adds here is that the practice of dialogue in education is demanded not merely on pedagogical grounds but also for profound philosophical and theological reasons: *the very nature of human life is characterized by dialogical communication with God, nature, and other persons.*

Freire's views on God-human relationships can be gathered from the false notions about God that he subjects to criticism. He often criticizes a *magical view* of God according to which persons believe that God, especially a punishing God, can be controlled by magical beliefs and rituals.[11] To transcend such magical notions is one of the primary purposes of Freire's process of conscientization. Freire often connects such magical beliefs and mentality with poor peasants. In describing the thinking of peasants in northeast Brazil, he states that they are unable to arrive at a structured view of the world or understand the reasons for their plight. The peasant looks for causes in things higher and more powerful. "One such thing is God, whom he sees as the maker, the cause of his condition. Ah, but if God is responsible, man can do nothing."[12] Freire recognizes that many now react against this attitude since they have begun to accept the truth

> that we have to earn our heaven here and now. We have to build our heaven, to fashion it during our lifetime, right now. Salvation is something to achieve, not just something to hope for.[13]

Freire rejects the notion that God is responsible for oppression with these strong words: "How could we make God responsible for this calamity? As if Absolute Love could abandon man to constant victimization and total destruction. That would be God as described by Marx."[14]

Freire also attacks the myth that rebellion is a sin against God, a myth which, he contends, even many of the oppressed share, when they ascribe their pitiful situation to the will of God.[15] This myth, internalized by oppressed people, prevents them from seeing an act of rebellion against oppression as a warranted and justified confrontation with their human destiny. As discussed in an earlier chapter, what Freire approves here is a concept of God that includes God's deep involvement in human history, even to the point of encouraging acts of revolution and rebellion. This is no doubt a controversial view of God, yet the image of the Warrior God is a powerful one among religious groups that attempt to deal with oppressions, as the Jewish people involved in their exodus and their return from captivity.

Freire does accept the concept of *God as Savior*, but he makes some interesting points about this doctrine. He states that we do not save ourselves alone but in communion with others. In his view

> you don't save me, because my soul, my being, my conscious body is not something that A and B can save. We work out our salvation in communion. I don't mean that God hasn't saved us by His presence in history; I'm talking now on the human level.[16]

Freire's discussion of salvation is always in these worldly terms which never assert or deny a salvation beyond this life. What he is insistent upon, with many liberation theologians, is that the Christian life is lived in communion.

JESUS CHRIST

Freire does not make many references to Jesus in his writings, and when he does, he refers to him as Christ. In speaking about the prophetic church which challenges injustices in society, he states that "Christ was no conservative. The prophetic church like him, must move forward constantly, forever dying and forever being reborn."[17]

Freire refers to the doctrine of the incarnation as establishing the principle that the starting point of theology has to be humanity: "But as a matter of fact, just as the Word became flesh, so the Word can be approached only through man. Theology has to take its starting point from anthropology."[18]

Freire's most profound statements about Jesus are included in the use he makes of the "Easter experience." As explained earlier, conscientization is interpreted as an experience of dying and rising, denouncing and announcing. For Freire, "every Christian must live his Easter, and that too is utopia. The man who doesn't make his

Easter, in the sense of dying in order to be reborn, is no real Christian."[19] Freire presents himself as a person who continues to live this experience.

WORD OF GOD

The symbol of the word is a powerful one in Freire's writings. His literacy programs are concerned with generative words, that is, words which not only generate other words but which also generate a new level of political consciousness in adult learners. The goal of education is to enable persons to speak their own words to the world. The human word for Freire is not merely language; it is also action. Words are not just something spoken; they are also something to be done.

Given this understanding of word in his general theory, it is interesting to analyze his treatment of the important religious symbol of the word of God. For Freire, to know the word of God is to both hear the word and to put it into practice. Consequently one cannot know God's word unless one is first dedicated to human liberation through concrete actions. According to Freire, "in the final analysis the word of God is inviting me to re-create the world, not for my brother's domination but for liberation."[21] Hearing entails willingness and commitment to live the word fully.

Preaching and hearing the Word of God is not to be understood in a banking sense of making and receiving deposits. We are not vessels who wait to be filled by this word as if it is a pourable substance and we are passive recipients. The word of God is liberating and saving only when we make ourselves active in working for salvation and liberation. In Freire's schema, the reason why the word of God is heard especially in the Third Word is that in this world there occurs the Easter experience of dying and resurrecting.

Freire stresses that the chief response to the word of God is not only individual but, more importantly, group conversion. He rejects the view that to transform the world it is sufficient to change minds and hearts while leaving social structures unchallenged. In his view, exhortations, good works, and intellectualizing are not adequate to this task. Only active involvement in politics will lead to the radical transformation of social structures that is called for in situations of oppression.[21]

For Freire, the fact that the word of God became flesh means that God's word can only be approached through our actual life with our brothers and sisters. Thus the incarnation provides an anthropological starting point not only for theology but for Christian life in the world. Reading the word, reading the Gospels, demands communion and commitment with brothers and sisters.

THEOLOGY OF THE CHURCH

In a number of chapters I have made reference to the important article by Freire, "The Educational Role of the Churches," and its companion article, "Education, Liberation, and the Church."[22] These articles that contain Freire's views on the church are, in his own estimation, important for understanding his more mature thought.

Of course, Freire does not present a full ecclesiology. His concern is, as always, with explaining the type of education that he accepts and rejects. Yet in doing so he does indicate what his thinking is about the nature and mission of the Christian churches.

Freire makes the point that the only way to discuss the church is to treat it not as an abstract entity but as *an institution involved in history*. For this reason the churches cannot be neutral but must take a stand or make judgments on problems that a particular society faces. For example, the churches cannot wash their hands of the problems of excessive political and economic power in the hands of an elite. Freire also argues against the the naive or moralistic attitude of those who feel that it is sufficient for churches to use sermons on otherworldy values to change the world. The attitudes of the neutralists and the moralisers, in his opinion, serve the interests of the dominant ruling classes. Under the guise of defending the faith they defend class interests.

Freire challenges the churches to become utopian and prophetic. They become this by denouncing injustices in the world and announcing a more just world to be brought about through historical-social praxis of the oppressed. If churches do not become prophetic and utopian, they become formalist, bureaucratic, alienated, and alienating.

Freire calls *leaders* of the churches to *"experience their own Easter"* by dying to elitist attitudes and by resurrecting on the side of the oppressed. Changed consciousness is not enough to accomplish this; what is called for is involvement in praxis with the oppressed to transform the world. In other words, it is not just talk and purely palliative attitudes that are demanded, but active political involvement. Freire recognizes that a different type of theological education will have to be provided for leaders of a utopian or prophetic church.

In describing three types of churches—traditionalist, modernizing, and prophetic—Freire makes a connection with his theories about levels of consciousness and types of education. Though these types of churches have been discussed in an earlier chapter, a brief repetition may serves to present a full picture of Freire's theological views. The *traditionalist church,* which is caught up in a semi-intransitive consciousness, receives severe criticism from Freire for its colonialist mentality. It places emphasis on sin, hell fire, and eternal damnation. Human life is presented as an ordeal we must experience in order to achieve heaven. Viewing the world as a basically evil place, these churches preach an otherworldly salvation. Freire is highly critical of these churches for their alignment with the ruling powers.

Modernizing churches, characterized by naive consciousness, are institutions that attempt to adopt modern means of fostering religious life and managing religious organizations. For example, they utilize social workers, make use of mass media, and develop methods of planning and evaluation. Yet for Freire these churches do not go far enough to confront the real problems that many societies face. The attitude that these churches take toward capitalism is a primary example for Freire. Rather than condemning capitalism, they attempt to humanize it. Not recognizing that a class society is at the heart of the struggle for transforming society, churches allow this situation to go without criticism and challenge.

Freire praises *prophetic churches,* places where leaders and people have achieved critical consciousness. These churches engage in a critical analysis of society and commit themselves to radical social change on behalf of the oppressed. These churches, which are involved in a new Exodus, have emerged in many parts of the Third World and can be termed truly revolutionary. Examples of prophetic churches for Freire are the basic Christian communities prevalent in his native Brazil.

THEOLOGY AND POLITICS

It is clear from what has been said that Freire creates a tie between theology and politics. Freire treats this relationship in a review of James Cone's *Black Theology of Liberation*.[23] Freire sees a relationship between black theology and Latin American liberation theology in that both have a political nature. Both of these theologies are aligned with the struggles of oppressed groups to speak their own word, to make history, to participate in revolutionary praxis.

Both black and Latin American theology do not shrink from advocating political action out of any fear of offending theological purity. Freire agrees with Cone's contention that white theology is political in that it defends the class interests of the dominant white class. White theology is charged with attempting to reconcile things which cannot be reconciled, denying class differences, and sanctioning only modernizing efforts in society. To the oppressed this theology preaches about the value of suffering, sacrifice, resignation, and purification of sins.

Freire praises the politization of theology fostered by Cone's black theology of liberation. He praises it for directing the oppressed not to submit to suffering but to transform it into a faith that "can give meaning to the future, not as an alienating vagueness or as a predetermined entity, but as a task of construction, a deed of liberty."[24]

OTHER INFLUENCES OF FREIRE ON LIBERATION THEOLOGY

A Utopian Theology.

Latin American liberation theologians have taken note of the work of Paulo Freire. Gustavo Gutierrez has high praise for Freire's pedagogy of the oppressed. He refers to nonalienating and liberating cultural action which links theory with praxis in order to transform relationships with the world and other people. Gutierrez recognizes that Freire's ideas are in the development stage and refers to certain limitations in the process of conscientization, though he does not mention any specific limitations. Gutierrez notes with approval one element of Freire's analysis of Latin American society, a fixation which leads many Latin Americans to overvalue the past. This fixation, which is a manifestation of precritical consciousness, prevents the new person and the new society from emerging. Finally, he also notes Freire's description of the utopian process of denunciation of a unjust reality and the annunciation of a just reality, which he incorporates into his own concept of utopia and political action.[25]

Conscientizing Evangelization

Juan Segundo, another liberation theologian, draws from Freire his concept of conscientizing evangelization. In this form of evangelization the gospel is viewed as a liberating interpretation of history in which men and women are the subjects rather than the objects of history. If this method is not used, evangelizing and catechesis become not cultural action but cultural invasion, that is, the teaching of new words and ideas from another culture which do not correspond to the realities of life and which do not deal with the real alienations of people arising from fear, enslavement, and ideology. Segundo argues that the "intimate and necessary connection between evangelization and political conscientization . . . destroys any false hope of an aseptic evangelization."[26] Of the connection between literacy training and evangelization Segundo writes:

> An evangelization committed to man's liberation is deeply tied up with the new form of literacy training, i.e., one incorporated within a process of consciousness-raising. This new form of literacy training, as a process of liberation, possesses an educational technique in the service of man that is completely similar to those of the evangelization process. We should not even think of two different processes but of one single moment for the gradual liberation of man within which is included evangelization.[27]

Sacraments.

Freire's pedagogy has also been utilized to interpret the sacraments or ritual actions of the church. Drawing on Freire, Segundo explains the sacraments as a communitarian pedagogy of liberation. The object of these celebrations is not to make deposits of grace, which seems to be alienating magic, but to enable Christians to speak their own words. Segundo describes what should happen in the celebration of a sacrament:

> On the occasion of each sacrament it should present the Christian
> people with the present, concrete, existential situation. It should pose
> this situation as a problem that challenges them and calls for their
> response. And it should also show divine revelation to be an element
> capable of helping them face up to this challenge.[28]

The celebration of sacraments, to be a conscientizing experience,
should include both intellectual understanding and action, for
"when the Christian community organizes itself in sacramental
terms, it orients itself toward action designed to meet an historical
challenge in a reflective and critical way."[29] Segundo has no hesita-
tion in taking over statements from Paulo Freire, "simply replacing
such terms as *literacy training,* education and culture with their
corresponding terms in our discussion, i.e., *sacraments, grace, the
Christian task,* etc."[30]

Freire and Basic Christian Communities

On a number of occasions Freire has made reference to the
basic Christian communities in Brazil. These communities are small
groups of Christians who meet to discuss the scriptures in order to
apply them to the concrete problems of their lives.

Freire recounts that these communities originated in Brazil in
the early 1960's. He speaks of the activity of these communities
during the years of the military regime as efforts of individuals and
groups to defend themselves against despotic rule. In his view liberation theology began within these groups which provided a fellowship of defense, an intimacy in the church. He contends that

> when popular groups assume the role of subjects in studying the
> Gospels, which they no longer simply read, then they inevitably
> study them from the standpoint of the oppressed and no longer from
> that of the oppressor.[31]

These communities, according to Freire, are examples of prophetic
churches that in taking on political tasks do not lose a faith
dimension.

While Freire does not speak of his own influence on these
communities, others have made the connection.[32] Freire's pedagogy
or method of conscientization is utilized in many of these communities, which from the very beginning have used his method as an
interpretive tool for reflection on the Bible at their weekly prayer
and worship.

Theological Method

The case has been made that Freire's method of conscientization is the method for liberation theology.[33] Although there no
doubt are similarities between the two approaches, there does not
appear to be any direct adoption of conscientization by major Latin
American theologians. Gutierrez has described the method of liberation theology as critical reflection on praxis in light of the word of
God. Theologians of liberation make participation in the struggles
of the oppressed a precondition for doing theology.

McCann has made the point that the Freire method is not an
adequate method for theology since it rejects tradition and authority
in its extreme open-endedness. There is no doubt some justification
in Freire's writing for this viewpoint. He does seem to indicate that
all truths are open to revision. Yet McCann may be bringing to this
discussion some presuppositions about the nature of religious truths
and their unchanging character. Freire clearly puts himself on the side
of change. This is understandable given the context of his writings, a
situation in which an almost fatalistic attitude was taken toward
religious truth. However, his emphasis on the total openness to religious truths does not mean that for him all truths are of equal value
or that there is not value to religious traditions and authority.

NOTES

1. Paulo Freire. "A Letter to a Theology Student." *Catholic Mind,*
   Vol. LXX, No. 1265, 1972, p. 8.
2. Paulo Freire. *The Politics of Education.* South Hadley, Mass.:
   Bergin and Garvey, 1985, p. 127.
3. Paulo Freire. "A Letter to a Theology Student," p. 7.
4. Paulo Freire. "Conscientizing as a Way of Liberating." LADOC.
   1972, II. 29a, p. 8. This is a taped version of a talk given by Freire
   in Rome in 1970.
5. Paulo Freire. "A Letter to a Theology Student," p. 7.
6. Paulo Freire. "A Letter to a Theology Student," p. 9.
7. Paulo Freire. *La educacion como pratica de la libertade.* Santiago, Chile: ICIRA, Calle Arturo Claro, p. 15. This passage has
   been omitted from the English translation, *Education for Critical Consciousness.*

8. Paulo Freire. *The Politics of Education,* p. 103.
9. Paulo Freire. "A Letter to a Theology Student," p. 1.
10. Paulo Freire. *Education for Critical Consciousness.* New York: Seabury, 1973, p. 18.
11. Paulo Freire. *Education for Critical Consciousness,* pp. 103–104.
12. Paulo Freire. "Conscientization." In Walter Conn, ed. *Conversion.* New York: Alba House, 1977, p. 303.
13. Paulo Freire. "Conscientization." p. 304.
14. Paulo Freire. "Conscientization." p. 304.
15. Paulo Freire. *Pedagogy of the Oppressed.* New York: Seabury, 1970, pp. 136, 163.
16. Paulo Freire. "Conscientization." p. 306.
17. Paulo Freire. *The Politics of Education,* p. 139.
18. Paulo Freire. "A Letter to a Theology Student," p. 7.
19. Paulo Freire. "Conscientization." p. 306.
20. Paulo Freire. "A Letter to a Theology Student," p. 7.
21. Paulo Freire. "The Educational Role of the Churches in Latin America" Washington, D.C.: LADOC, 3, 14, 1972, p. 15.
22. Paulo Freire. "The Educational Role of the Churches in Latin America." "Education, Liberation, and the Church." *Risk,* Vol. 9, no. 1, 1973, pp. 34–38.
23. Paulo Freire. *The Politics of Education,* pp. 145–150.
24. Paulo Freire. *The Politics of Education,* p. 146.
25. Gustavo Gutierrez. *Theology of Liberation.* Maryknoll, New York: Orbis Books, 1973, pp. 91–92.
26. Juan Segundo. *The Idea of God.* Maryknoll, New York: Orbis Books, 1974, p. 174.
27. Juan Segundo. *The Idea of God,* pp. 174–175.
28. Juan Segundo. *The Sacraments Today.* Maryknoll, New York: Orbis Books, 1970, p. 104.
29. Juan Segundo. *The Sacraments Today,* p. 104.
30. Juan Segundo. *The Sacraments Today,* p. 101.
31. Paulo Freire and Antonio Faundez. *Learning to Question: A Pedagogy of Liberation.* New York: Seabury, 1989, p. 66.
32. Alfred Hennelly. *Theology for a Liberating Church.* Washington, D.C.: Georgetown University Press, 1989, pp. 28, 81.
33. Dennis McCann. *Christian Realism and Liberation Theology.* Maryknoll, New York: Orbis Books, 1981, chapter 7.

Epilogue

Paulo Freire is without a doubt one of the most significant educators of the latter part of the twentieth century. His work is known in all parts of the world. Scholars have probed the multiple aspects of his writings: philosophy, theology, social theory, political theory and education. Practitioners have utilized his methods not only in literacy education but also in community organization and social action.

The question is: will Paulo Freire's work remain significant in the next century? I believe that it will. Wherever people suffer oppression and wherever educators are motivated to help remove the causes of oppression, Freire's work will have a prominent place. Notwithstanding the many criticisms that his work has received, no one can fail to be moved by the passion, intelligence, and commitment that permeates all of his work, especially *Pedagogy of the Oppressed.*

The forms of oppression that Freire addressed were primarily economic. If present events are any harbinger of things to come, the next century will be marked additionally by fierce religious and ethnic oppressions. Freire's optimistic philosophy of human nature will be needed to counter growing pessimism. His vision of a society dedicated to the humane value of freedom, equality, and fraternity will stand as a challenge to all state forms of repression.

Freire's work will continue to be a remarkable and classic statement about the power of education to address in a realistic manner the social problems of the times. His abiding message is that there is hope for mankind as long as a people are free both to be educated and to educate. Through giving the world a noteworthy pedagogy of the oppressed, he may indeed become for all generations a pedagogue of liberation.

References

Althusser, Louis. *For Marx*. New York: Random House, 1970.

Arendt, Hannah. *The Origins of Totalitarianism*. Meridian Books, 1958.

Arendt, Hannah. *On Revolution*. The Viking Press, 1963.

Arraes, Miguel. *Brazil: The People and the Power*. Middlesex, Eng.: Penguin Books, 1969.

Ashton-Warner. Sylvia. *Teacher*. New York: Simon and Schuster, 1963.

Barnard, Clift. "Imperialism, Underdevelopment and Education." In Robert Mackie, ed., *Literacy and Revolution: The Pedagogy of Paulo Freire*. New York: Continuum, 1981, pp. 12–38.

Bee, Barbara. "The Politics of Literacy." In Robert Mackie, ed. *Literacy and Revolution: The Pedagogy of Paulo Freire*. New York: Continuum, 1981.

Berger, Peter, and Luckmann, Thomas. *The Social Construction of Reality*. Garden City, N. Y.: Doubleday, 1966.

Berger, Peter. *Pyramids of Sacrifice*. Baltimore: Penguin, 1977.

Bowers, C. A. *Elements of a Post-Liberal Theory of Education*. New York: Teachers College Press, 1987.

Brinton, Crane. *The Anatomy of a Revolution*. Rev. ed. New York: Random House, 1965.

Collins, Denis, *Paulo Freire: His Life, Works, and Thought*. New York: Paulist Press, 1977.

Cox, Harvey. *The Secular City*. New York: Macmillan, 1965.

Cox, Harvey . *Religion in the Secular City*. New York: Simon and Schuster, 1984.

Debray, Regis. *Revolution in the Revolution*. Grove Press, 1967.

de Kadt, Edward. *Catholic Radicals in Brazil*. London: Oxford University Press, 1970.

Dewey, John. *Democracy and Education*. New York: Macmillan, 1917.

Diuguid, Leo H. "Brazil Wages Two-pronged War on Illiteracy." *The Washington Post,* Section D-3, December 20, 1970.

Donohoe, John W. "Paulo Freire—Philosopher of Adult Education." *America,* Vol. CXXVII, No. 7, 1972.

Dulles, John H. *Unrest in Brazil.* Austin, Texas: University of Texas Press, 1970.

Elias, John L. *Conscientization and Deschooling: Freire's and Illich's Proposals for Reshaping Society.* Phila.: Westminster, 1976.

Egerton, John. "Searching for Freire." *Saturday Review of Education,* Vol. 1, No. 3, 1973.

First Encounter of Christians for Socialism: The Final Document. Washington, D. C.: LADOC, 3, 8a, 1973.

Frankena, William K. "A Model for Analyzing a Philosophy of Education." In J. Martin, ed., *Readings in the Philosophy of Education,* Boston: Allyn and Bacon, 1970, pp. 15–22.

Freire, Freire. *La Educacion Como Pratica de la Libertade.* Santiago, Chile: ICIRA, Calle Arturo Claro, 1967.

Freire, Paulo. *Education as the Practice of Liberty.* Rio de Janeiro: Paz e Terra, 1967.

Freire, Paulo. *Pedagogy of the Oppressed.* New York: Seabury, 1970.

Freire, Paulo. *Cultural Action for Freedom.* Cambridge, Mass.: *Harvard Educational Review* and Center for the Study of Development and Social Change, 1970.

Freire, Paulo. "Conscientizing as a Way of Liberating." LADOC. 1972, II. 29a, p. 8. This is a taped version of a talk given by Freire in Rome in 1970.

Freire, Paulo. "The Educational Role of the Churches in Latin America." Washington, D.C.: LADOC, 3, 14, 1972.

Freire, Paulo. "A Letter to a Theology Student." *Catholic Mind,* Vol. LXX, No. 1265, 1972.

Freire, Paulo. *Education for Critical Consciousness.* New York: Seabury, 1973.

Freire, Paulo. "Education, Liberation, and the Church." *Risk,* Vol. 9, no. 1, 1973, pp. 34–38.

Freire, Paulo. "Conscientization." In Walter Conn, ed. *Conversion.* New York: Alba House, 1977, p. 303.

Freire, Paulo. *Pedagogy in Process: The Letters to Guinea-Bissau.* New York: Seabury, 1978.

Freire, Paulo , "When I met Marx I continued to meet Christ on the corner of the street," in *The Age* Newspaper, Melbourne, Australia, April 19, 1974, quoted in Robert Mackie, *Literacy and Revolution: The Pedagogy of Paulo Freire.* New York: Continuum, 1981, p. 126.

Freire, Paulo. *The Politics of Education: Culture, Power, and Liberation.* Granby, Mass.: Bergin and Garvey, 1985.

Freire, P., and Macedo, D. *Literacy: Reading the Word and the World.* South Hadley, Mass.: Bergin and Garvey, 1987.

Freire, Paulo. "The People Speak their Word: Literacy in Action." In Paulo Freire and Donaldo Macedo. *Literacy: Reading the Word and the World.* South Hadley, Mass.: Bergin and Garvey, 1987.

Freire, Paulo, and Faundez, Antonio. *Learning to Question: A Pedagogy of Liberation.* New York: Continuum, 1989.

Freyre, Gilberto. *The Masters and the Slaves.* New York: Knopf, 1964.

Fromm, Erich. *Escape from Freedom.* Boston: Holt, 1941.

Giroux, Henri. "Introduction" to Paulo Freire. *The Politics of Education.*

Gramsci, Antonio. *Cultura y literatura.* Madrid: Ediciones Peninsula, 1967.

Guttierez, Gustavo. *Theology of Liberation.* Maryknoll, New York: Orbis Books, 1973.

Heilbroner, Robert. *Between Capitalism and Socialism.* New York: Random House, 1970.

Hennelly, Alfred. *Theology for a Liberating Church.* Washington, D.C.: Georgetown University Press, 1989.

Horowitz, Irving L. *Three Worlds of Development: The Theory and Practice of International Stratification.* New York: Oxford University Press, 1966.

Houtart, Francois, and Rousseau, Anton. *The Church and Revolution.* Maryknoll, New York: Orbis Books, 1971.

Johnson, Chambers. *Revolutionary Change.* Boston: Little Brown and Co., 1966.

Juliao, Francisco. *Combao—The Yoke, the Hidden Face of Brazil.* Middlesex, Eng.: Penguin Books, 1972.

Kolakowski, Leszek. *Towards a Marxist Humanism.* New York: Grove Press, 1968.

McCann, Dennis. *Christian Realism and Liberation Theology.* Maryknoll, New York: Orbis Books, 1981.

McClellan, James E. *Toward an Effective Critique of American Education*. Phila.: Lippincott, 1968.

Mackie, Robert, ed. *Literacy and Revolution: The Pedagogy of Paulo Freire*. New York: Continuum, 1981.

Mannheim, Karl. *Ideology and Utopia*. New York: Harcourt, Brace & World, 1966.

Popper, Karl. *The Open Society and Its Enemies*. Princeton: Princeton University Press, 1983.

Rawls, John. *A Theory of Justice*. Cambridge, Mass.: Harvard University Press, 1971.

Sanders, Thomas G. "Brazil: A Catholic Left." *America,* Vol. CXVII, 1967, pp. 598–601.

Segundo, Juan. *The Sacraments Today*. Maryknoll, New York: Orbis Books, 1970.

Segundo, John. *The Idea of God*. Maryknoll, New York: Orbis Books, 1974.

Skidmore, Thomas. *Politics in Brazil 1930–1964: An Experiment in Democracy*. New York: Oxford University Press, 1967.

Shor, Ira, and Freire, Paulo. *A Pedagogy for Liberation: Dialogues on Transforming Education*. South Hadley, Mass.: Bergin and Harvey, 1987.

Wagley, Charles, *An Introduction to Brazil*. New York: Columbia University Press, 1971.

Weffort, Francisco. "Education and Politics." Introduction to Paulo Freire, *Education as the Practice of Freedom*. Cambridge, Mass.: Center for the Study of Development and Social Change, 1969.

INDEX OF PRINCIPAL NAMES

INDEX OF PRINCIPAL SUBJECTS

VITA

Dr. John L. Elias is Professor of Religion and Education at Fordham University. He has lectured extensively in the United States and Great Britain on educational and theological issues. His publications include *Philosophical Foundations of Adult Education, Foundations and Practice of Adult Religious Education, Psychology and Religious Education, Studies in Theology and Education,* and *Moral Education: Secular and Religious.* As director of Fordham's Center for Education in Peace and Justice, Dr. Elias works with community groups and churches in developing forms of liberating education.